June 12, 2005

With love from
your family at
Trinity U.C.C.

Advice for achieving your goals
from remarkably successful people

SUCCESS

J. Pincott, editor

Random House Reference
New York · Toronto · London · Sydney · Auckland

Please address inquiries about electronic licensing of any products for use on a network, in software or on CD-ROM to the Subsidiary Rights Department, Random House Information Group, fax 212-572-6003.

This book is available for special discounts for bulk purchases for sales promotions or premiums. Special editions, including personalized covers, excerpts of existing books, and corporate imprints, can be created in large quantities for special needs. For more information, write to Random House, Inc., Special Markets/ Premium Sales, 1745 Broadway, MD 6-2, New York, NY, 10019 or e-mail *specialmarkets@randomhouse.com*.

Visit the Random House Reference Web site: *www.randomwords.com*

Library of Congress Cataloging-in-Publication Data

Success : advice on achieving your goals from remarkably successful people / J. Pincott, editor.—1st ed.
    p. cm.
  Includes bibliographical references.
ISBN 0-375-42589-6
1. Success—Quotations, maxims, etc.   I. Pincott, J. (Jena)

PN6084.S78S84 2005
646.7—dc22

2005043202

First edition

Printed in the United States of America

10 9 8 7 6 5 4 3 2
ISBN: 0-375-42589-6

INTRODUCTION

This book, a collection of advice and inspiration on how to be successful, celebrates self-made men and women. I've scoured autobiographies, interviews, commencement speeches, and other sources to see what the Oprah Winfreys, Bill Gateses, J.K. Rowlings, Ray Krocs, David Sedarises, Pablo Picassos, and Madeleine Albrights say about their successes—and how their experiences might apply to you. Most of the CEOs, Nobel Prize winners, politicians, academics, entrepreneurs, and celebrities quoted here are successful because they skillfully leveraged ambition, talent, knowledge, and hard work. They picked up a few tips and techniques along the way and are open about their discoveries.

The advice and anecdotes excerpted in this book suggest that the "secrets of success" are in some ways transferable. They can be used by anyone. Success isn't sorcery.

It wasn't always so. Take for example the Chamberlains, a family of 17th century male midwives. At a time when mothers and babies often died during childbirth, the Chamberlains magically delivered one healthy baby after another. Mothers-to-be were blindfolded so they wouldn't see the forceps, the obstetrical tool that the Chamberlains invented. The Chamberlains kept their secret under wraps, literally, working under sheets that hid their hands. To further obscure their secret, they allegedly transported the forceps in a massive and mystical gold box.

Today, in America and throughout much of the world, success is associated with hard work and temperament more than with magic, divine right, or a blessed bloodline. Successful people find themselves encouraged—*strongly* encouraged—to talk about their experiences and dispense advice and know-how.

Some of the excerpts in *Success* focus on specific actions ("Work out all the steps of the process—the entire, what, when, where, and how. Then, sit down after you are absolutely positive you know it cold, and write it out."—Michael Bloomberg). Most of the quotes emphasize the attitudes and ideas that made success possible

("If you can connect yourself to the source and allow the energy that is your personality, your life force, to be connected to the greater force, anything is possible for you."—Oprah Winfrey).

I have loosely organized the excerpts by theme; for example, "Setting Your Goals," "Getting Started," "Working with Others," and "Projecting Your Image." I have emphasized career success over, say, spiritual success or success in relationships (although there are crossovers into these areas). Career success here is not limited to success that manifests itself in abundant wealth or celebrity (although examples of this are certainly included). I have featured artists, poets, scientists, CEOs, and others who have had extraordinary careers but haven't become household names.

Although *Success* is not a how-to manual—there are no concrete rules for success—my hope is that you will use it to help realize your goals. Use it for inspiration and light guidance. Perhaps, like forceps in the delivery room, this tool will make the process a little easier.

CONTENTS

For some people, success is simply defined: it's the act of accomplishing something one has set out to do. But finishing something isn't always the same as being successful at it. For many, success also implies meaningfulness and magnitude. Almost every person has his or her own definition of success—and many of these definitions are anything but definite.

It's worthwhile to think about what success means to you and what it means to others. And it's up to you to decide if you want the latter to influence the former.

DEFINING SUCCESS

Can success change the human mechanism so completely between one dawn and another? Can it make one feel taller, more alive, handsomer, uncommonly gifted and indomitably secure with the certainty that this is the way life will always be? It can and it does!
—**Moss Hart**, *playwright*

❧

Success is a consequence and must not be a goal.
—**Gustave Flaubert**, *writer*

❧

Success is a science; if you have the conditions, you get the result.
—**Oscar Wilde**, *playwright*

❧

SUCCESS AS QUALITY OF LIFE

In the most general sense, success may be defined by the quality of the life you lead and the model you set for others.

Be the change you want to see in the world.
—*Mahatma Gandhi,* Indian nationalist leader

This is the one true joy in life, the being used for a purpose recognized by yourself as a mighty one; the being thoroughly worn out before you are thrown on the scrap heap; the being a force of nature instead of a feverish little clod of ailments and grievances complaining that the world will not devote itself to making you happy.
—*George Bernard Shaw*, playwright

To laugh often and much; to win the respect of intelligent people and the affection of children; to earn the appreciation of honest critics and endure the betrayal of false friends; to appreciate beauty, to find the best in others; to leave the world a little better; whether by a healthy child, a garden patch or a redeemed social condition; to know even one life has breathed easier because you have lived. This is the meaning of success.
—*Ralph Waldo Emerson,* poet and
philosopher (attributed)

∽

Look up the word success in ten different dictionaries and you will get ten different definitions. *Webster's New World Dictionary* defines success as, quote, The gaining of wealth, fame, etc. End quote.

If that definition is correct, what word should we use to describe the men and women who pour their hearts into their careers. . . . Who devote their entire lives to raising bright and honest children. . . . Who give generously to their community and live model lives? Are we to conclude that they are good and decent people, but not successful people? . . . Not by my standards—and, I hope, not by yours . . . To me, success is merely the process of fulfilling your own hopes and dreams—not by the standards set by *society*—but by the standards set by *you*.

—*George Pataki,* governor of New York

To me success is the ability to love and to have compassion. It's the capacity to experience joy and spread it to others. It's the security of knowing that your life has meaning and purpose. It is a sense of connection to the creative power of the universe. It's also the ability to fulfill your goals. It's the progressive realisation of worthy goals. It's also the expansion of happiness. When you have all that, then material success in terms of material acquisitions and comforts and luxury, follows as a by-product.

—**Deepak Chopra**, *writer, medical doctor, and CEO of the Chopra Center*

WHAT YOU DO DEFINES YOU

Playwright Arthur Miller was keenly aware of the assumption that success in life means success in what you do for a career.

❧

Success, instead of giving freedom of choice, becomes a way of life. There's no country I've been to where people, when you come into a room and sit down with them, so often ask you, "What do you do?" And, being American, many's the time I've almost asked that question, then realized it's good for my soul not to know. For a while! Just to let the evening wear on and see what I think of this person without knowing what he does and how successful he is, or what a failure. We're ranking everybody every minute of the day.

—**Arthur Miller**, *playwright*

❧

Success is the space one occupies in the newspaper.
—**Elias Canetti**, writer and philosopher

FINDING YOUR PURPOSE

Career success must start with the act of defining one's purpose in life—which sounds simpler than it is.

I'm convinced that business success in the future starts with the question, What should I do with my life? Yes, that's right. . . . People don't succeed by migrating to a "hot" industry (one word: dotcom) or by adopting a particular career-guiding mantra (remember "horizontal careers"?). They thrive by focusing on the question of who they really are—and connecting that to work that they truly love (and, in so doing, unleashing a productive and creative power that they never imagined).

—*Po Bronson,* writer, in *What Should I Do With My Life?*

∽

Unless that underground level of the self is preserved as a verified and verifying element in your makeup, you are going to be in danger of settling into whatever profile the world prepares for you and accepting whatever profile the world provides for you. You'll be in danger of molding yourselves in accordance with laws of growth other than those of your own intuitive being.

—*Seamus Heaney,* poet

THE RIGHT ATTITUDE

Many equate success with simply having an attitude that makes success possible. Success is mindset.

If you can conceive it and believe it, you can achieve it.

—*Rev. Jesse Jackson,* civil rights leader, minister, and politician

∾

Don't give in.

Fight for your future.

Independence is the only solution.

Women are as good as men.

Onward!

You don't have too much money but you do have independent spirits. Knowledge! Education!

Don't give in! Make your own trail.

Don't moan.

Don't complain.

Think positively.

—*Katharine Hepburn,* actor

All successful men have agreed in one thing—they were causationists. They believed that things went not by luck, but by law; that there was not a weak or a cracked link in the chain that joins the first and last of things. A belief in causality, or strict connection between every trifle and the principle of being, and, in consequence, belief in compensation, or, that nothing is got for nothing—characterizes all valuable minds, and must control every effort that is made by an industrious one. The most valiant men are the best believers in the tension of the laws.

—**Ralph Waldo Emerson**, *poet and philosopher*

What is success? I think it is a mixture of having a flair for the thing that you are doing; knowing that it is not enough, that you have got to have hard work and a certain sense of purpose.

—**Margaret Thatcher,** former prime minister of Great Britain

∽

There are two kinds of success, or rather two kinds of ability displayed in the achievement of success. There is, first, the success either in big things or small things which comes to the man who has in him the natural power to do what no one else can do, and what no amount of training, no perseverance or willpower, will enable any ordinary man to do. This success, of course, like every other kind of success, may be on a very big scale or on a small scale. The quality which the man possesses may be that which enables him to run a hundred yards in nine and three-fifths seconds, or to play ten separate games of chess at the same time blindfolded, or to add five columns of figures at once without effort, or to write the "Ode to [sic] a Grecian Urn," or to deliver the Gettysburg speech, or to show the ability of Frederick at Leuthen or Nelson at Trafalgar . . . This is the most striking kind of success, . . . But much the commoner type of success in every walk of life and in every species of effort is that which comes to the man who differs from his fellows not by the kind of quality which he possesses but by the degree of development which he has given that quality. This kind of success is open to a large number of persons, if only they seriously determine to achieve it. It is the kind of success which is open to the average man of sound body and fair mind, who has no remarkable mental or physical attributes, but who gets just as much as possible in the way of work out of the aptitudes that he does possess. It is the only kind of success that is open to most of us. Yet some of the greatest successes in history have been those of this second class—when I call it second class I am not running it down in the least, I am merely pointing out that it differs in kind from the first class. To the average man it is probably more useful to study this second type of success than to study the first. From the study of the first he can learn inspiration, he can get uplift and lofty enthusiasm. From the study of the second he can, if he chooses, find out how to win a similar success himself. I need hardly say that all the successes I have ever won have been of the second type. I never won anything without hard labor and the exercise of my best judgment and careful planning and working long in advance.

—*Theodore Roosevelt,* U.S. president

THE ROLE OF LUCK

There are always contrarians and coy celebrities who define their success to a combination of many ineffable things, mainly luck.

I feel that I've been completely lucky. That if I didn't have a talent to amuse people, I would have scuffled to have some kind of job, I don't know what. I would have done the best I could. Instead, due to some quirk of nature, I was able to make jokes and be amusing. I've led a very, very privileged life and out of pure luck. I'm the first one to say it. I feel personally that, in a number of ways, I really haven't lived up to the luck that I've had. I've tried my best to, but I wish I had achieved better things than I've done. But I'm totally cognizant of the fact that I've just been completely lucky.

—**Woody Allen,** *director, producer, and writer*

Whatever success I have I owe, as does anyone, to a combination of luck, genetics, ambition, and perhaps a slight admixture of application.
—**David Mamet,** author and playwright

If one is lucky, a solitary fantasy can totally transform one million realities.
—**Maya Angelou,** poet

When I work fourteen hours a day, seven days a week, I get lucky.
—**Armand Hammer,** founder and president of Occidental Petroleum

Success is simply a matter of luck. Ask any failure.
—**Earl Wilson,** journalist

Excellence and indifference rarely mix. If your only motivation is to fulfill another person's expectations of you, or simply to make money, chances are that you won't be a great success. If you're blasé about what you do, hard work and long hours may yield little but exhaustion. You may try to convince yourself that a love of fame or wealth is enough to achieve success in a field that bores you, but you probably won't be able to believe it for long.

FINDING YOUR
PASSION

The secret of success is
making your vocation your vacation.
—**Mark Twain**, *writer, journalist,*
and humorist

Success is not the key to happiness.
Happiness is the key to success. If you love
what you are doing, you will be successful.
—**Albert Schweitzer**, *humanitarian,*
theologian, and medical doctor

A man is a success if he gets up in the
morning and gets to bed at night, and in
between he does what he wants to do.
—**Bob Dylan**, *musician*

I'd rather be a failure at something I enjoy
than be a success at something I hate.
—**George Burns**, *actor and comedian*

FOLLOW YOUR IDEA OF FUN

Most people would agree that happiness and fulfillment is part of success. Think of the top three things you enjoy doing. What excites you? What can you imagine doing every day?

People rarely succeed unless they have fun in what they are doing.

—*Andrew Carnegie,* industrialist and philanthropist

Enthusiasm is one of the most powerful engines of success. When you do a thing, do it with all your might. Put your whole soul into it. Stamp it with your own personality. Be active, be energetic, be enthusiastic and faithful, and you will accomplish your objective. Nothing great was ever achieved without enthusiasm.

—*Ralph Waldo Emerson,* poet and philosopher

For other than the choice of a lifetime partner, nothing determines happiness so much as choosing the right kind of work. It is a choice about what is good for you, not what is good for others whom you greatly respect—your parents, an admired professor, your friends, a significant other, any or all of whom you suspect may be dazzled by a greater or loftier choice of profession. The choice is not about what makes them happy, but about what makes you happy. Not what seems to show that you are successful by the exterior measurements of the society. Not about what brings you the biggest salary—particularly in the beginning when those things seem so important—and the biggest house, or the greatest respect from Wall Street, but what makes you feel complete and happy and makes you feel, for this is no small thing, like a part of something larger than yourself, a part of a community. In the end this is a choice you must make for yourself, for no one can make it for you.

—*David Halberstam,* journalist, writer, and historian

I think I've cared less about "how can I be more like XXXX" than about just trying to do what I think is fun, interesting, and right. Motto in life: "Do unto others what you would like others to do unto you. And have fun doing it."

—*Linus Torvalds,* founder of Linux

Apple Computer CEO Steve Jobs has enlightened many misguided minds that believe success can be derived of anything but passion. The price of success is simply too high if you're uninspired.

A lot of people come to me and say, "I want to be an entrepreneur," And I go, "Oh that's great, what's your idea?" And they say, "I don't have one yet." And I say, "I think you should go get a job as a busboy or something until you find something you're really passionate about because it's a lot of work." I'm convinced that about half of what separates the successful entrepreneurs from the nonsuccessful ones is pure perseverance. It is so hard. You put so much of your life into this thing. There are such rough moments in time that I think most people give up. I don't blame them. It's really tough and it consumes your life. . . . It's pretty much an eighteen-hour day job, seven days a week for a while. Unless you have a lot of passion about this, you're not going to survive. You're going to give it up. So you've got to have an idea, or a problem or a wrong that you want to right that you're passionate about, otherwise you're not going to have the perseverance to stick it through. I think that's half the battle right there.

—*Steve Jobs*, cofounder and CEO of
Apple Computer

Bon Jovi was not supposed to succeed. Ask any critic. We weren't from N.Y. We weren't from L.A. I didn't live the cliché rock 'n' roll lifestyle that "legends" were made of. We tried to keep up with the Joneses until I realized that even if you win the rat race, you're still a rat. One out of every 1,000 bands gets a record deal. One out of a million have any success. I've been to the top and I've been written off more than once . . . but I'm still here. Still the underdog? Maybe. Passionate? Definitely. Nothing is as important as passion. No matter what you want to do with your life, be passionate. The world doesn't need any more gray. On the other hand, we can't get enough color. Mediocrity is nobody's goal and perfection shouldn't be either. We'll never be perfect. But remember these three P's: Passion + Persistence = Possibility.

—*Jon Bon Jovi,* musician

༝

. . . Love what you do, or don't do it. Don't *make a choice of any kind, whether in career or in life, just because it pleases others or because it ranks high on someone else's scale of achievement or even because it seems to be, perhaps even for you at the time, simply the logical thing to do at that moment on your path. Make the choice to do something because it engages your heart as well as your mind. Make the choice because it engages all of you.*

—**Carleton (Carly) Fiorina,** *former chairman and CEO of Hewlett-Packard*

༝

. . . One of the things my dad kept instilling in me was the joy of the game. He made it fun for me. A lot of the times I see a lot of the kids; they don't enjoy being out there, and that's a shame, you're supposed to enjoy the game . . . I think that's one of the things I've learnt from my father and what I try to instill in all my clinics is yes, go out there and give it all you have, but more importantly, enjoy what you're doing . . .

—**Tiger Woods,** golfer

Larry Page and Sergey Brin, creators of the search engine Google, simply wanted to do what they love: work with computers. For them, from that, success came easily.

> I think part of the reason we're successful so far is that originally we didn't really want to start a business. We were doing research at Stanford University. Google sort of came out of that. And we didn't even intend to build a search engine originally. We were just interested in the Web and interested in data mining. And then we ended up with search technology that we realized was really good. And we built the search engine. Then we told our friends about it and our professors. Pretty soon, about 10,000 people a day were using it.
>
> —*Larry Page,* cofounder of Google

Matt Damon and Ben Affleck wrote their box office hit *Good Will Hunting* without any expectation of success. They did it simply because they were passionate about moviemaking.

> We wrote it right out of frustration. It was like, Why are we sitting here? Let's make our own movie. And if people come to see it, they come; and if they don't, they don't. Either way it beats sitting here going crazy. When you have so much energy and so much passion and no outlet for it and nobody cares, it's just the worst feeling.
>
> —*Matt Damon,* actor, producer, and screenwriter

. . . There's sort of a more selfish angle that I just HAVE to write songs, almost to even the pressure out. It's like if I create a song, then I have a replica outside me of what I'm hearing inside, and it sort of evens out the pressure. That is quite a physical, almost selfish, thing and it's as important to me as it is to eat or sleep.

—Björk Gudmundsdóttir, *singer*

PICK YOUR PASSION—
OR LET IT PICK YOU—BUT DON'T
LET OTHERS PICK IT FOR YOU

Most of the earth's inhabitants work to get by. They work because they have to. They didn't pick this or that kind of job out of passion; the circumstances of their lives did the choosing for them. Loveless work, boring work, work valued only because others haven't got even that much, however loveless and boring—this is one of the harshest human miseries.

—*Wislawa Szymborska,* Nobel Prize winner for Literature

Undertaking a certain career only to please your parents, spouse, or others may make you dutiful but not successful.

. . . One's task consists first of all in mastering a life that is one's own, not imposed or prescribed from without, no matter how noble its appearance may be. For each of us is issued but one life, and we—know full well how it all ends. It would be regrettable to squander this one chance on someone else's appearance, someone else's experience.

—*Joseph Brodsky,* Nobel Prize winner for Literature

. . . I had this passion—this dedication to be something—to do something with my writing. I'm very proud to flip back to my blue and white annual, when I graduated from L.A. High School in summer, 1938, when I was seventeen years old. They asked me how I was going to predict my future. And underneath my picture, I had them put, "Headed for Literary Distinction." How in the hell did I know that? How in the hell did I know that—because I was nowhere, I was nowhere at all. And the last night at school, I went up on top of the school—it was sunset, and I was playing a part in a play—and I cried. Because I knew it was going to be years before anything happened to me. But I had to make it happen. I had to make it happen. I had to believe in my passion. So, that's the way it finally turned out.

—**Ray Bradbury**, *writer*

I've never remembered a time when I wasn't in love with calculating. One of the first memories I have was when I was still being put down for a nap in the afternoons. I was in the crib and not able to climb out, and I was calculating the infinite series, $1 + \frac{1}{2} + \frac{1}{4} + \frac{1}{8} + \frac{1}{16} \ldots$ and discovered that it came out to $2. \ldots$ I just loved calculating. It's something you're born with . . . .

—*Freeman Dyson*, physicist

. . . I slowly saw that not only was I not free, but my brothers and sisters were not free. I saw that it was not just my freedom that was curtailed, but the freedom of everyone who looked like I did. That is when I joined the African [National] Congress, and that is when the hunger for my own freedom became the greater hunger for the freedom of my people. It was this desire for the freedom of my people to live their lives with dignity and self-respect that animated my life, that transformed a frightened young man into a bold one, that drove a law-abiding attorney to become a criminal, that turned a family-loving man into a man without a home, that forced a life-loving man to live like a monk.

—*Nelson Mandela*, former president of South Africa and Nobel Peace Prize laureate

MONEY IS NOT ENOUGH

Don't conflate the pursuit of success with the pursuit of wealth. Riches alone may not compensate for the misery of an unhappy profession. Success transcends dollars and cents.

The American admiration for success is totally braided with the idea that if you make money, that's good. And if you do something that has no financial reward, then there's something very peculiar, or you've made some incredible mistake.

—*Susan Sontag,* writer and activist

. . . Though [money is] crucial to make a living, that shouldn't be your inspiration or your aspiration. Do it for yourself, your highest self, for your own pride, joy, ego, gratification, expression, love, fulfillment, happiness—whatever you want to call it. Do it because it's what you have to do. And if you make this music for the human needs you have within yourself, then you do it for all humans who need the same things. Ultimately, you enrich humanity with the profound expression of these feelings.

—*Billy Joel,* musician

. . . Fulfill all your values as a human being in the work place. If you are an activist, bring the activism of your life into your business, or if you love creative art, you can bring that in. If I had learned more about business ahead of time, I would have been shaped into believing that it was only about finances and quality management. There is a sort of terrorism that comes with the operations and the science of making money, but by not knowing any of that, I had an amazing freedom.
—**Anita Roddick**, founder of The Body Shop

Money isn't the thing that drives me. When I look at a project, I'm not thinking about the paycheck. I only look at the character I would play, the script, and whether I think it could work out to be a good film.
—**Keanu Reeves,** actor

Love your work. If you always put your heart into everything you do, you really can't lose. If your heart is in it, you'll probably succeed, and if it isn't in it, you probably won't succeed. But the reason you can't lose is that whether you wind up making a lot of money or not, you will have had a wonderful time, and no one will ever be able to take that away from you . . . I used to be afraid that writing and acting in comedies might be a frivolous occupation, but when I think about all the good that laughing does for people, I get the feeling that making people laugh can be noble work . . .
—**Alan Alda,** writer, director, and actor

I thought I was going to make crazy cartoons for the rest of my life. I didn't think I'd ever get paid for it, didn't think I drew well enough, but I knew it made me happy.
—**Matt Groening,** creator of *The Simpsons*

Success simplified: First, identify your interests. Second, establish a goal. Third, achieve it. Unfortunately, it can be extremely difficult to just get from steps one to two. You may not have an idea yet of exactly what you want to do. Or perhaps you do, but your ambition is too vague to act on. Or maybe your interests are specific yet too overwhelming. Any number of catalysts might work for you: role models, restlessness, reading, research, etc. Try them all.

GETTING STARTED

❦

Whatever your ambitions, whatever the field you want to enter, if you want to play a game go to where it's played. If you want to be a lawyer, go to law school. If you can't get into the best law school, get into the best one you can. Same with medical or business school or whatever. If you want to get into TV, get yourself a job, any job in the business. The important thing is to get your seat at the table.
—Christopher Matthews,
television news journalist, commentator

❦

The most difficult thing is the decision to act, the rest is merely tenacity. The fears are paper tigers. You can do anything you decide to do. You can act to change and control your life; and the procedure, the process is its own reward.
—Amelia Earhart, *aviator*

❦

SYNTHESIZE

One way to get started is to think about all the things you've experienced that fascinate you—your hobbies, travel, academic classes, etc. Tap into these passions and let them flow together. Perhaps your interests are pop psychology, silent films, and gourmet cooking. Dream up ways in which your interests might inform one another and lead to a completely unique venture—a business, a book, a new approach to your current work.

I get a lot of my ideas from synthesizing things from different disciplines. It might be something from the world of technology, it might be something from the world of retailing or the grocery business or it might be something really just from reading. I read many hours a week, all kinds of different things, a lot of things on business and very little fiction, although a little bit. So I get a lot of ideas from there and I think I get a lot of ideas from the other members of our senior management team.
—*Frederick W. Smith,* founder, president, and CEO of FedEx

START WITH SOMETHING, ANYTHING

Imagine that you have a blank canvas in front of you. How do you begin the masterpiece that represents your goal? Start with something, anything—a few brushstrokes or sketches. You'll benefit from the momentum.

✍

. . . When I'm in the harrowing phase and feel restless, it means I'm ready to start, that I must start, that I can begin the film. And initially I need to observe, to meet people with simplicity, as happens on a bus or a train; I need to sketch. I reflect, observe some details, a tic, a gesture, a color, a face.

—**Federico Fellini,** *filmmaker and director*

✍

> How wonderful it is that nobody need wait a single moment before starting to improve the world.
> —**Anne Frank,** diarist

INVOKE INSPIRATION

Nikola Tesla, inventor of the polyphase alternating current electricity (the basis of our modern electrical system), developed a visualization exercise that would fire his creativity. This is how he invoked inspiration and ideas:

. . . I instinctively commenced to make excursions beyond the limits of the small world of which I had knowledge, and I saw new scenes. These were at first very blurred and indistinct, and would flit away when I tried to concentrate my attention upon them. They gained in strength and distinctness and finally assumed the concreteness of real things. I soon discovered that my best comfort was attained if I simply went on in my vision further and further, getting new impressions all the time, and so I began to travel; of course, in my mind. Every night, (and sometimes during the day), when alone, I would start on my journeys—see new places, cities and countries; live there, meet people and make friendships and acquaintances and, however unbelievable, it is a fact that they were just as dear to me as those in actual life, and not a bit less intense in their manifestations. This I did constantly until I was about seventeen, when my thoughts turned seriously to invention. Then I observed to my delight that I could visualize with the greatest facility. I needed no models, drawings or experiments. I could picture them all as real in my mind. Thus I have been led unconsciously to evolve what I consider a new method of materializing inventive concepts and ideas, which is radically opposite to the purely experimental and is in my opinion ever so much more expeditious and efficient.

—*Nikola Tesla,* physicist and inventor

Allow inspiration to hit you. This is how Sylvia Nasar conceived *A Beautiful Mind*, her best-selling biography of mathematician John Nash:

> While working on an economics piece for the [*The New York*] *Times*, about a year and a half before Nash got the Nobel, I heard a rumor that a mathematical genius who had suffered from schizophrenia for three decades might be on a short list for the prize. I thought, "Oh my God, this sounds like a Greek tragedy, Shakespeare play and fairy tale rolled into one."

—*Sylvia Nasar,* writer

How J.K. Rowling conceived Harry Potter:

> My boyfriend was moving to Manchester and wanted me to move, too. It was during the train journey back from Manchester to London, after a weekend looking for a flat, that Harry Potter made his appearance. I have never felt such a huge rush of

excitement. I knew immediately that this was going to be such fun to write. . . . I didn't know then that it was going to be a book for children—I just knew that I had this boy, Harry. During that journey I also discovered Ron, Nearly Headless Nick, Hagrid, and Peeves. But with the idea of my life careering round my head, I didn't have a pen that worked! And I never went anywhere without my pen and notebook. So, rather than trying to write it, I had to think it. And I think that was a very good thing. I was besieged by a mass of detail and if it didn't survive that journey it probably wasn't worth remembering.
—*Joanne Kathleen (J.K.) Rowling*, writer

Stress may actually help inspire you. It helped Walt Disney find the inspiration to conceive Mickey Mouse:

Mickey Mouse popped out of my mind onto a drawing pad 20 years ago on a train ride from Manhattan to Hollywood at a time when business fortunes of my brother Roy and myself were at lowest ebb and disaster seemed right around the corner.
—*Walt Disney*, founder of Walt Disney, Inc.

For singer and songwriter Enya, inspiration is a place.

Many things inspire me when I am composing, most of which come from thoughts I have about special moments in my life—from memories, from my childhood, from my family, and from people I know from the landscapes of my native Gaothdobhair. Gaothdobhair is very beautiful; it is in the Northwest coast of Ireland, set against the Atlantic Ocean. The name translates as "Plain of the Winds," which may give you some idea of its character.

—*Eithne Ní Bhráonain (Enya),* singer

For writer Paul Auster, inspiration is coming up with the perfect title of a book.

I find it impossible to start a project without the title in mind. I can sometimes spend years thinking of the title to go with the thing that's forming in my head. A title defines the project somehow and if you keep finding the ramifications of the title in the work it becomes better, I'm convinced of this. So, yeah, I think about titles a lot. Sometimes I just walk around making up titles for things that don't exist, and never will exist.

—*Paul Auster,* writer

FIND A PROBLEM
THAT NEEDS A SOLUTION

If your interests are too vague, one effective way to focus yourself may be to find a problem to solve or a way to improve something in some way. If you can find the solution, you'll also find success.

> Pick a problem based on how much you care about it. However impenetrable it seems, if you don't try it, then you can never do it. Always try the problem that matters most to you.
> —*Andrew Wiles,* mathematician

> Problems are only opportunities in work clothes.
> —*Henry J. Kaiser,* industrialist

The inventor of e-mail was looking for a better way to communicate.

> It [e-mail] was a hack—a neat thing to try out. . . . It probably took four, five, six hours to do. Less than a day spread over a week or two—when I had a spare moment.
> —*Ray Tomlinson,* computer scientist

The founder of Craigslist was looking for a better way to get people to share listings of apartments, jobs, secondhand items, dates, and such.

> We address everyday human needs, and do a great job of it. People find the site [Craigslist] very useful, and promote the site to their friends and family via word of mouth. When someone has a positive experience on the site, they tend to bring in those around them as well. We have never done any advertising and our growth via word of mouth has allowed us to be very successful. Also, we have seen the press be very kind to us.
>
> —*Craig Newmark,* founder and chairman of *Craigslist.org*

Scott Heiferman, founder of Meetup.com, identified a need for a tool to help people organize face-to-face meetings on topics from knitting to futurism to politics.

... Our growth has been driven by the simple fact that we have built something that people want to use. Generally the things that people gravitate towards are things they want.
—*Scott Heiferman,* founder of Meetup.com

You can also find a solution in search of a problem. eBay enjoys sustained success because its founders discovered an unprecedented way to take advantage of the Internet: provide a global service for online auctions.

> First, we created a business that took unique advantage of the properties of the Net—the Net's ability to connect many to many—allowing a business to be created where there was no land-based analog. If you can't buy your book at Amazon, you can still go down to Barnes & Noble. eBay has no land-based analog— not in one place. It was a business model that was created out of the technology called the Internet. Some of the most successful companies are those that had an entirely new model that could not have existed without the Net. eBay might be one of the only businesses that was created on the Internet.
>
> —*Meg Whitman*, president and CEO of eBay

Sometimes you don't need to *seek* a problem that needs a solution. It will come to you. Jonas Salk discovered the polio vaccine out of an urgent need to eradicate the crippling disease.

> You never have an idea of what you might accomplish. All that you do is you pursue a question. And see where it leads.
>
> —*Jonas Salk*, physician research scientist, and developer of the polio vaccine

FIND ROLE MODELS

Another way to get started is to seek out role models in your given field. For example, if you want to get started in comedy, find role models who are comedians.

> Here's one way: Get a job at a local comedy club as a waiter—or anything. Observe other comedians as much as you can—even down to studying the way they walk on- and offstage. See how they approach their material and what their attitude it. What will your attitude be when you walk up to the mike? Should it be joyous? Should it be troubled? Figure out what attitude fits you best.
>
> —*Rodney Dangerfield,* comedian and actor

Many successful people are cross-disciplinary, which means that you can—and should—be inspired by people in completely different fields. Fictional heroes are OK, too.

> My 4th and 5th grade teacher was a real inspiration to me—just that she seemed to care about students so much. It was at the time that my other hero, my father, was teaching me the values of education—why children have to learn to make this a better world than the parents had made and why school is so important to your life. I decided I wanted to be an engineer like my father, and second, I wanted to be a 5th grade teacher. Another hero was Tom Swift, in

the books. What he stood for, the freedom, the scientific knowledge and being an engineer gave him the ability to invent solutions to problems. He's always been a hero to me. I buy old Tom Swift books now and read them to my own children. Bob Dylan was a hero for early folk songs and the like. Just the way he put words together—strong meaning of very few words—just like trying to build a very good computer with very few parts.

—*Stephen Wozniak (Woz)*, engineer, teacher, and cofounder of Apple

I tell my [playwriting] students, not only should you know everything anybody else has ever written, you should know the bad stuff as well as the good. Because you don't want to be influenced by the bad stuff. You should also note the history of classical music, since you're writing stuff that is to be spoken and heard; and since you're also working with visual images, you should know about painting and sculpture.

—*Edward Albee*, playwright

MAKE GOOD FRIENDS

Find inspiration in the people you know who are leading a life that resembles the one you want. They may also beome your alliances throughout your career.

∽

My advice [to people who want to go into film] *is to find people your own age who are incredibly talented—filmmakers your own age, writers your own age, other actors—because they gravitate to action. Talented people ultimately find something to do. So you create circles of talent. . . .The real alliances are with the people you came up with. The ones in your generation. When you date upward that's not an alliance, because the other person has more power than you have. But the people you broke in with, if you don't lose them when you begin to get work, if you stay true to each other, those are people who will go to war with you.*

—**Lynda Obst,** director

∽

Don't make friends who are comfortable to be with. Make friends who will force you to lever yourself up.
—**Thomas J. Watson,** founder of IBM

BE OPPORTUNISTIC

If an opportunity comes around, know when to take it.

> There is a tide in the affairs of men,
> Which, taken at the flood, leads on to Fortune;
> Omitted, all the voyage of their life
> Is bound in shallows and in miseries.
> On such a full sea are we now afloat,
> And we must take the current when it serves,
> Or lose our ventures.
> —**William Shakespeare,** playwright, in *Julius Caesar*

Salesman Ray Kroc capitalized on two amazing opportunities. The first one was the Multimixer, a milkshake machine. The second was a restaurant that successfully used Multimixers. Building on his success as a Multimixer salesman, he eventually bought the restaurant and built a franchise on it. The restaurant's name: McDonald's.

After sixteen years of selling paper cups for Lily Tulip Cup Company, and climbing to the top of the organization's sales ladder, I saw opportunity appear in the form of an ugly, six-spindled milkshake machine called a Multimixer, and I grabbed it. It wasn't easy to give up security and a well-paying job to strike out on my own. My wife was shocked and incredulous. But my success soon calmed her fears and I plunged gleefully into my campaign to sell Multimixers to every drugstore fountain and dairy bar in the nation. It was a rewarding struggle. I loved it. Yet I was alert for other opportunities. I have a saying that goes, "If you're green you're growing, as soon as you're ripe you start to rot. And I was as green as a Shamrock shake on St. Patrick's Day when I heard of an incredible thing that was happening with my Multimixer out in California [at the McDonald's restaurant that he would eventually buy].

—*Ray Kroc*, founder of McDonald's Corp.

When Stanley Kaplan got his first look at an SAT test in 1946, he immediately saw a business opportunity. Coaching students on standardized tests would become a multimillion dollar business in the years to come.

I looked at the sample questions, and a broad smile stretched across my face. It was love at first sight. . . . For instance, one question asked, "Approximately 820 tons of water per second fall over each of the 11 gates if the Grand Coulee Dam. If the same total amount of water were to fall over only 5 gates, how many tons per second would fall over each gate? I could see that the questions were designed to test students' knowledge and application of basic concepts, not their ability to regurgitate memorized facts. There were no pat answers. . . . As I scanned the information booklet, my eye glanced at a statement that said "cramming or last-minute reviewing" had no purpose and was not advised. I remember thinking, "Not review for a test?" Now I was really interested.

—*Stanley Kaplan,* founder of Stanley H. Kaplan Educational Centers

Sheeraz Hasan, now a successful Bollywood filmmaker, knew that chance favors a prepared mind. His opportunity came in the form of an office building where he had access to big Hollywood players.

Arriving in Los Angeles, I decided to surround myself with the movers and shakers in the business. To do this, I moved into an office complex called Lantana in Santa Monica. Here I was in the same office as [Steven] Spielberg, Jennifer Lopez, Chris Tucker, Catherine Zeta-Jones, Harrison Ford, and many more industry executives. While rubbing shoulders with the biggest players in Hollywood, I realised that to make it here, I would need a niche. While talking to the studio heads and celebrities in my office, I was often asked about Bollywood. Most people knew little about Bollywood and were unaware of its size and success. I then realised that if I could bring the two biggest film industries together, I would achieve something truly unique.

—*Sheeraz Hasan,* CEO, producer, and television host

START EVEN WHEN
STARTING IS INCONVENIENT

The bottom line is that you need to start somewhere—and you'll never know if you're going in the right direction until you take a step. There may never be a good time to get started. Your task is to make time, even if it's just a half hour each day.

I was not only working full-time, I was going to evening classes to get the professional qualification in hospital administration. I was visiting my husband in hospital on the weekend, and when the children were home, of course I was with them. It was just that I realized that there was never going to be a convenient time to start that first novel, and if I didn't make time, find the motivation, I would be a failed writer and that would be absolutely appalling for me.

—*Phyllis Dorothy (P.D.) James,* writer

I know other people who would never feel that they were a writer as long as they had another job, but I never felt that way. You meet people who say, "Oh, I'd like to do such-and-such, but I don't have the time." But it always seemed to me like you make the time. And if you have a wife or a job, if you have kids or whatever, you find a way. If you really want to do it, you make the time. When you have nothing but time, it's not nearly as satisfying.
—**David Sedaris**, writer and comedian

Now that you know what you want to do and you have some momentum, what happens next? Sadly, passion alone won't guarantee success—especially if it is unfocused, misapplied, and squandered. To be successful, you will need to set goals. Just don't look for consensus about how detailed your goals must be. Some successful people rely on intricately structured steps toward exacting goals; others insist that too much structure can be limiting and tip the balance away from creativity and passion. Find a medium that works for you.

SETTING YOUR GOALS

Our goals can only be reached through a vehicle of a plan, in which we must fervently believe, and upon which we must vigorously act. There is no other route to success.
—Pablo Picasso, *artist*

Give me a stock clerk with a goal and I'll give you a man who will make history. Give me a man with no goals and I'll give you a stock clerk.
—James Cash (J.C.) Penney, *founder of J.C. Penney*

UNDERSTAND THE PSYCHOLOGY OF GOAL-MAKING

Goal-making is a means to an end. The long-term vision required to identify a goal is a crucial part of success. Goals make accomplishments meaningful. They invigorate the process. They provide definition and direction and help launch your success.

Goals provide the energy source that powers our lives. One of the best ways we can get the most from the energy we have is to focus it. That is what goals can do for us; concentrate our energy.

—*Denis Waitley*, motivational speaker

A man has to have goals—for a day, for a lifetime—and that was mine, to have people say, 'There goes Ted Williams, the greatest hitter who ever lived.'

—*Ted Williams*, baseball player

If you don't set goals, you're not going to have dreams, either. The goals are the achievements along the way to get you to your dreams. . . . The longer you wait to decide what you want to do, the more time you're wasting. It's up to you to want something so badly that your passion shows through in your actions. Your actions, not your words, will do the shouting for you.

—*Derek Jeter*, baseball player

SEE THE BIG PICTURE

How ambitious should your goal be?

My goal is simple. It is a complete understanding of the universe, why it is as it is and why it exists as all.
—*Stephen Hawking*, physicist

ℳ

The substance of your goals may be secondary to their size. Believe Big. The size of your success is determined by the size of your belief. Think little goals and expect little achievements. Think big goals and win big success. Remember this, too! Big ideas and big plans are often easier—certainly no more difficult—than small ideas and small plans.
—*David Joseph Schwartz*, motivational speaker

ℳ

Success is about creating value. And it doesn't matter whether you're financing a new company, launching a brand online, raising a daughter, or scaling a mountain—the process of creating value requires some specific steps.

First, imagine what you want to see in the world—something that doesn't exist. Then take out a blank sheet of paper and design it. It could be a company, a product, a garden—anything. Second, inspire the

people around you to become comfortable with the concept of "filling the blank page." Do this by example and by experiment. Third, stick with it through the hard times. You will learn that they are the best teachers. You will also learn that they are inevitable.
—*Candice Carpenter,* CEO of iVillage

Start with a dream. Maybe a dream that is personal and small, but worth doing. Then dream a bigger dream. Keep dreaming until your dreams seem impossible to achieve. Then you'll know you're on the right track. Then you'll know you're ready to conjure up a dream big enough to define your future and perhaps your generation's future.
—*Vance Coffman,* chairman and CEO of Lockheed Martin

Consult not your fears but your hopes and your dreams. Think not about your frustrations, but about your unfulfilled potential. Concern yourself not with what you tried and failed in, but with what it is still possible for you to do.
—*Pope John XXIII*

We [Coldplay] want to be the best band of all time. Of course that sounds ridiculous, but that really is the force that drives us, and we might never get there, but it's a good force to have driving you 'cause it means that we want to work harder and harder and harder. I'm sure most bands want to be the best band in the world, but we really do.

—*Chris Martin,* musician

For people who are less certain about where they want to end up, another tactic is to set goals that point you in a *general* direction, allowing for maximum flexibility. For example, back in college, filmmaker George Lucas had no idea he would end up where he did. He just believed that by focusing on his studies and interests, he'd go somewhere.

Part of the issue of achievement is to be able to set realistic goals, but that's one of the hardest things to do because you don't always know exactly where you're going, and you shouldn't. For me, just setting the goals of getting decent grades in school and taking subjects I had some interest in was a big goal, and I focused on that.

—*George Lucas,* filmmaker

BREAK YOUR GOAL DOWN INTO STEPS

Many successful people talk about making a hierarchy of their goals. First, they identify their ultimate goal or goals—for example, becoming the managing director at an investment bank and a good mother. Then they break their dream down into manageable steps. Many successful people say they do something *every day* that applies to their ultimate goal.

Goals are dreams with deadlines.
—*Diana Scharf Hunt,* aphorist

In his autobiography, *My Life,* former president Bill Clinton reveals that when he graduated from law school he read a how-to book, *How to Get Control of Your Time and Your Life* by Alan Lakein. That's when he prioritized his life goals.

The book's main point was the necessity of listing short-, medium-, and long-term life goals, then categorizing them in order of their importance, with the A group being the most important, the B group next, and C the last, then listing under each goal specific activities designed to achieve them. . . . I do remember the A list. I wanted to be a good man, have a good marriage and children, have good friends, make a successful political life, and write a great book.
—*William (Bill) Clinton,* U.S. president

At every stage of his career, from bodybuilder to movie star to politician, Arnold Schwarzenegger defined his goals, collapsed them into manageable daily tasks, and relentlessly followed through.

∽

The most important thing is that you see your goal in front of you. You always have to see it in front of you, because that will become the motivating force for you. If you want to be a champion in something, or let's say that your goal is to be the police chief of your town, you should always have that in front of you, because at every move you make throughout the day, you can ask yourself, 'Will this get me to my goal, or will it deviate from the plan? . . . Every set that I did in the gym, every repetition I did on chin-ups or on squats with 500 pounds, I never said to myself, 'Oh my God, another rep.' I said, 'Yes! Another rep, another rep,' because that will make my dreams turn into reality.

—Arnold Schwarzenegger, *actor and governor of California*

∽

Andrew Wiles, the mathematician who devoted years of his life to trying to solve Fermat's Last Theorem, a famous mathematical puzzle, compares the step-by-step process of attaining his goal to exploring a dark mansion room-by-room.

You enter the first room of the mansion and it's completely dark. You stumble around bumping into the furniture, but gradually you learn where each piece of furniture is. Finally, after six months or so, you find the light switch, you turn it on, and suddenly it's all illuminated. You can see exactly where you were. Then you move into the next room and spend another six months in the dark. So each of these breakthroughs, while sometimes they're momentary, sometimes over a period of a day or two, they are the culmination of—and couldn't exist without—the many months of stumbling around in the dark that precede them.

—**Andrew Wiles**, *mathematician*

ADD OR SUBTRACT STEPS
WHEN NECESSARY

Michael Bloomberg founded Bloomberg L.P., a multimedia empire that focuses on financial information. Later in his career, he became the mayor of New York City. He advises against detailed plans that might bog a person down, but he does insist on working out the steps toward a goal. Most of all, he emphasizes the need to be flexible when planning.

Think logically and dispassionately about what you'd like to do. Work out all the steps of the process—the entire, what, when, where, and how. Then, sit down after you are absolutely positive you know it cold, and write it out. There's an old saying, "If you can't write it, you don't know it." Try it. The first paragraph invariably stops you short. "Now why did we want this particular thing?" you'll find yourself asking. "Where did we think the resource would come from?" "And what makes us think others—the suppliers, the customers, the potential rivals—are going to cooperate?" On and on, you'll find yourself asking the most basic questions you hadn't focused on before taking pen to paper.

As you discover you don't know it all, force yourself to address the things you forgot, ignored, overestimated, or glossed over. Write them down for some doubting stranger who doesn't come with unquestioned confidence in the project's utility—and who, unlike your spouse, parent, sibling, or child, doesn't have a vested interest in keeping you happy. Make sure your written description follows from beginning to end, in a logical, complete, double path.

Then tear up the paper.

That's right, rip it up. You've done the analysis. You've found enough holes in the pan to drive your hoped-for Bentley automobile through repeatedly. You've planned for myriad what-if scenarios. You've presented your ideas to others. You've even mapped out the first few steps.

But the real world throws curveballs and sliders every day, as well as the fastballs you practice against. You'll inevitably face problems different from the ones you anticipated. Sometimes you'll have to "zig" when the blueprint says "zag." You don't want a detailed, inflexible plan getting in the way when you have to respond instantly. By now, you either know what you can know—or you don't and never will. As to the rest, take it as it comes.

—**Michael Bloomberg**, founder and CEO of Bloomberg L.P. and mayor of New York City

↬

*. . . A large portion of success
is derived from flexibility.
It is all very well to have principles,
rules of behavior concerning
right and wrong. But it is
quite as essential to know when to
forget as when to use them.*

—**Alice Foote MacDougall**, entrepreneur

In writer Stephen Baxter's experience, his early goal of writing was trumped by a serious career in science, but later readopted when the serious science career wasn't to be.

I completed a Ph.D. in aeronautical engineering. But it wasn't for me; the detail tended to drive me crazy. I like research, but the bigger picture and wider aspects appeals more, not to mention communicating what I find. So after that I tried teaching—only to find no money or respect and maximum stress—and then about ten years in industry, working my way (not always consciously) towards a writing career, which if you'd asked me at about age 15 was always my goal, but which I thought was probably unreachable until it started happening.

—*Stephen Baxter,* writer

Actor Elizabeth Shue finished her Harvard degree 19 years after she started.

I went pretty consistently at first. I did two years at Wellesley and then I took two years off. Then I went a year straight at Harvard. Then I took a year off. Then I went to Harvard for another semester. Then I took 10 years off. Then I finally went back and finished that final semester. It's the best thing I've ever done in my life.

—*Elizabeth Shue,* actor

Your ultimate goal may only be achieved after you have experience doing other things, and some of these other things may seem superfluous to your goal. For Candace Bushnell, author of *Sex and the City*, the path to becoming an author wasn't straight and narrow.

When I was in my twenties, which was in the 1980s, nobody was interested in publishing anything that was about the life of a 20-something woman living in New York. Publishers really felt there was no market for it. I ended up being a journalist because I wanted to be a writer and I wanted to pay my rent. I'm glad to have had that experience. You learn a lot of discipline being a journalist, and, hah, they don't really care if you don't feel like doing it. . . . I do think that writing is a craft and it does take you about 20 years, I think. It's a commitment. Bret Easton Ellis said something really interesting which is true: People in their twenties don't see beginnings, middles, and ends. They see where they are and things that happen to them, but they don't have the perspective of how it fits into a bigger picture. Bret said that it wasn't until he got to be in his mid-thirties that he understood that things have beginnings, middles and ends.

—*Candace Bushnell*, writer

ॐ

Goals are a means to an end, not the ultimate purpose of our lives. They are simply a tool to concentrate our focus and move us in a direction. The only reason we really pursue goals is to cause ourselves to expand and grow. Achieving goals by themselves will never make us happy in the long term; it's who you become, as you overcome the obstacles necessary to achieve your goals, that can give you the deepest and most long-lasting sense of fulfillment.

—*Anthony Robbins,* motivational speaker and management consultant

What motivated you to choose your goal? What inspires you to succeed at it? What pushes you to keep trying? What carries you through times of self-doubt? Your answers to these questions comprise your character; they define your interests, values, strengths, and means of support. The stronger your character, the more stable your success.

CULTIVATING
CHARACTER

Watch your thoughts; they become words.
Watch your words; they become actions.
Watch your actions; they become habits.
Watch your habits; they become character.
Watch your character; it becomes
your destiny.
—**Frank Outlaw**, *actor*

Once you begin to understand, really
understand, how your thoughts create your
inner reality, and how that reality spills into
your world through your words and your
deeds, then you are on your way to trans-
forming them, and yourself. In order to live
a life of material and spiritual abundance,
everything about you must be in harmony.
—**Suze Orman**, *financial planner,*
writer, and speaker

Dogs got personality.
Personality goes a long way.
—**Quentin Tarantino**, *screenwriter and*
director, in Pulp Fiction

FIND A SOURCE OF
POWER AND CONVICTION

Some powerful people attribute their success to a greater power or life force.

> Self-trust is the first secret of success, the belief that if you are here the authorities of the universe put you here, and for cause, or with some task strictly appointed you in your constitution, and so long as you work at that you are successful.
> —*Ralph Waldo Emerson,* poet and philosopher

Larry Wall, creator of the popular computer programming language known as Perl, explains the link between his spiritual beliefs and his livelihood:

> . . . I think the universe is a pretty hefty inspiration for anyone who aspires to be a creator. I've certainly tried to put a universe of ideas into Perl, with some amount of success . . . For instance, the notion that you can change the world. The idea that other people are important. The love of communication and an understanding of rhetoric, not to mention linguistics. The appreciation of the importance of text. The desire to relate everything to everything else. The passion to build up rather than tear down.
> —*Larry Wall,* computer scientist

If you were to ask me what is the secret to my success, it is because I understand that there is a power greater than myself that rules my life and in life if you can be still long enough in all of your endeavors, the good times, the hard times, to connect yourself to the source, I call it God, you can call it whatever you want to, the force, nature, Allah, the power. If you can connect yourself to the source and allow the energy that is your personality, your life force, to be connected to the greater force, anything is possible for you. I am proof of that. I think that my life, the fact that I was born where I was born, and the time that I was and have been able to do what I have done speaks to the possibility. Not that I am special, but that it could be done. Hold the highest, grandest vision for yourself.

—**Oprah Winfrey**, talk show host

BE IN TOUCH WITH YOURSELF

Many successful people insist that it's necessary to look into oneself to find core values, intuition, "gut feeling," or an "inner voice." Depend on these for guidance.

Get to know yourself. Know your own failings, passions, and prejudices so you can separate them from what you see. Know also when you actually have thought through to the nature of the thing with which you are dealing and when you are not thinking at all. . . . Knowing yourself and knowing the facts, you can judge whether you can change the situation so it is more to your liking. If you cannot—or if you do not know how to improve on things—then discipline yourself to the adjustments that will be necessary.
—***Bernard M. Baruch,*** financier

❧

You will, undoubtedly, meet people who will try to shut you up or entice you to compromise your principles in any number of ways. They'll try to seduce you and distract you with money, power, security and perhaps, most dangerously, a sense of belonging. Don't let them; it's just not worth it. One of the biggest threats to our world is the culture of silence and compromise—politicians who compromise their beliefs because they're scared they'll piss off their voters and won't get reelected, corporate executives who put profits above principles. You can have a conscience and still make money. You can have genuine values and still get elected. You can even make movies that do well at the box office without playing to the lowest common denominator.

—*Samuel L. Jackson*, actor

Beware the irrational, however seductive. Shun the "transcendent" and all who invite you to subordinate or annihilate yourself. Distrust compassion; prefer dignity for yourself and others. Don't be afraid to be thought arrogant or selfish. Picture all experts as if they were mammals. Never be a spectator of unfairness or stupidity. Seek out argument and disputation for their own sake; the grave will supply plenty of time for silence. Suspect your own motives, and all excuses. Do not live for others any more than you would expect others to live for you.

—*Christopher Hitchens*, journalist

How will you succeed? The answer may be found in a few simple words written by Abe Lincoln: "When I do good I feel good. When I do bad I feel bad. And that's my religion." All of us have a voice inside that will speak to us if we let it. Sometimes it's easy to hear; sometimes we have to turn down the volume of the distracting noise around us so we can listen. That voice tells us if we are on the right track. It lets us know if we give as much as we take, if we welcome the opinions of others, and at least accept diversity even if we are not able to embrace it.

—**Christopher Reeve**, *actor*

Your past experience defines your character. Tap into a part of your past that has strengthened and inspired you. For actor and producer Harvey Keitel, it was his experience in the Marines.

> You know that saying, "Once a Marine, always a Marine?" I am still a Marine today. We shared this brotherhood of the spirit that to this day I feel, as do all former Marines. It lifted me, it elevated me, it spirited me, it challenged me to my limits, and my limits were extended. That helped me sustain a great deal of struggle I encountered on my road to becoming an actor.
>
> —*Harvey Keitel,* actor and producer

Surprisingly, artist Claude Monet also drew inspiration from his experiences in the military. He was conscripted when he was twenty and always regarded his seven years in the army as essential to his art.

> Nothing seemed more attractive than the endless trekking under the sun, the raids, the crackle of the gunpowder, the sabre-rattling, the nights spent under canvas in the desert and I imperiously waved aside all my father's objections. . . . I spent two really charming years in Algeria. There was always something new to see and in my spare time, I tried to capture what I saw. You cannot imagine the extent of

what I learned and how much my ability to see improved. I was not immediately aware of this. The impressions of light and colour that I gained there were, to some extent, put aside later, but the kernel of my future researches came from them.

—*Claude Monet,* artist

Radio talk show host Ira Glass talks about how he has attempted to suspend his adolescence for the sake of his work.

I feel when someone says that "sometimes adults act like adolescents," I almost feel there's a kind of negative spin in that sort of thing. "Why don't they act more adult?" But I feel that people who act like adolescents—they are the interesting people. Everything about being an adolescent, well, almost everything about it anyway, is the interesting thing about being a person. You feel you're on a process of discovery towards something. And you have things that you really love and you organize your life around things you really love.

—*Ira Glass,* radio talk show host

Howard Schultz, the visionary who popularized Starbucks, became a success by tapping into his past as a dreamy boy growing up in the projects of Brooklyn. He transformed the negative experience of poverty into an asset.

One thing I've noticed about romantics: They try to create a new and better world from the drabness of everyday life. That is Starbucks's aim, too. We try to create, in our stores, an oasis, a little neighborhood spot where you can take a break, listen to some jazz, or ponder universal or personal or even whimsical questions over a cup of coffee.

Who dreams up such a place?

From my personal experience, I'd say that the more uninspiring your origins, the more likely you are to use your imagination and invent worlds where everything seems possible.

That's certainly true of me.
—*Howard Schultz,* founder of Starbucks, Inc.

PROJECT YOURSELF INTO THE FUTURE

Where does this sense of self come from? After you have gained a long-term perspective by looking deep into your past, try to project yourself into the future—10 years, 30 years, 50 years from now. Some successful people swear this exercise really works.

> As a kid I wasn't very rich but when I went into the cosmetics business I wanted to make it very big. We were a tiny company, but I dreamed someday of being able to run a large company. . . . I came to realize that fantasizing, projecting yourself into a successful situation is the most powerful means there is of achieving personal goals. That is what an athlete does when he kicks a field goal with three seconds on the clock, and 80,000 people in the stands and 30 million people watching. As the kicker begins to move he automatically makes the thousand tiny adjustments necessary to achieve the mental picture he has formed in his mind so many times: the picture of himself kicking the winning field goal.
> —*Leonard Lauder,* president of Estée Lauder

By looking beyond the present, Amazon.com founder Jeffrey Bezos was able to leave his lucrative Wall Street job and pursue his dream of being an entrepreneur.

If you can project yourself out to age 80 and sort of think, "What will I think at that time?" it gets you away from some of the daily pieces of confusion. You know, I left this Wall Street firm in the middle of the year. When you do that, you walk away from your annual bonus. That's the kind of thing that in the short-term can confuse you, but if you think about the long-term then you can really make good life decisions that you won't regret later.

—*Jeffrey Bezos*, founder of Amazon.com

I want you all to look again upon your parents and grandparents and your stepparents. I want you to look real close and recognize yourself in them. And you know what? If you really don't see it because you're too lost in yourself, I want you to look a little closer or step a little further away. In full bloom and youth of life, take stock of time and the passing of time. And as you are promoted or demoted, as you purchase cars and computers and homes and trinkets and pay mortgages and alimony and child support, or not; as you skillfully scale the slippery slopes of success or fail as you gossip and backstab, and connive or remain stoically silent and advise; as you rush life away to get ahead or lazily slump and fall far behind, take stock of time.

—*Wynton Marsalis*, musician

EXPERIENCE ANOTHER
COUNTRY OR WAY OF LIFE

If it's possible for you, broaden your horizons by living abroad. If not, try other ways to experience how other people think and live. Visit other neighborhoods, join clubs, talk to strangers. Outside influences will make you more dynamic.

. . . Working or studying abroad—it's essential to success in our increasingly diverse world. Students with international exposure come to understand the value of dialogue between people from different cultures and between people with different points of view. They also gain an understanding of the importance of relationships. Relationships are the foundation for meaning and success in life.

—*Douglas Daft,* chairman and
chief executive of Coca-Cola

Learn at least one foreign language, or more if you have a talent for it. Look for opportunities to study, live, and work outside the United States. By immersing yourself in an entirely different culture, you'll be better prepared for the global culture that will dominate the 21st century.

—*Herbert Allison, Jr.,* former president and
CEO of Merrill Lynch & Co., Inc.

BE A GENERALIST

On the one hand, you need to focus on your goals in order to accomplish them. On the other hand, you must not limit yourself to doing one thing well and having an interest in only that one thing. Your sources of inspiration may come from unexpected places.

There's a lot of creative things that are related to each other and it definitely helps, going into a film, to have a lot of different experience in different areas. I'm more of a generalist than an expert on anything.

—*Sofia Coppola,* producer and screenwriter

. . . There is need for a person to be generally educated. Otherwise you shrivel up much too soon. Whether this means reading the Bible (I read the New Testament every few years) or reading the great 19th century novelists (the greatest and shrewdest judge of people and of society who ever lived), or classical philosophy (which I cannot read—it puts me to sleep immediately), or history (which is secondary). What matters is that the knowledge worker, by the time he or she reaches middle age, has developed and nourished a human being rather than a tax accountant or a hydraulic engineer . . . Otherwise, a few years later, tax accounting or hydraulic engineering will become awfully stale and boring.

—*Peter Drucker*, management theorist and writer

When you read or hear something, think about it and how it connects to everything else you know. This is how knowledge will become useful to you. Don't simply collect facts—you'll only forget them later because they aren't relevant to your life.

Most boys or youths who have had much knowledge drilled into them, have their mental capacities not strengthened, but overlaid by it. They are crammed with mere facts, and with the opinions or phrases of other people, and these are accepted as a substitute for the power to form opinions of their own: and thus the sons of eminent fathers, who have spared no pains in their education, so often grow up mere parroters of what they have learnt, incapable of using their minds except in the furrows traced for them. Mine, however, was not an education of cram. My father never permitted anything which I learnt to degenerate into a mere exercise of memory. He strove to make the understanding not only go along with every step of the teaching, but, if possible, precede it. Anything which could be found out by thinking I never was told, until I had exhausted my efforts to find it out for myself.

—*John Stuart Mill,* philosopher and economist

There's something dangerously solipsistic about our young people. They know less and less about the world around them. They know less and less about history. Of course, that's my generation's influence: We wanted to give them an education that seemed relevant to their lives, but the end result is that their education is specious and empty. Everything harsh has been removed from their education because we haven't wanted to upset them. But I say, let education give them the horrors so they don't have to get them from video games . . . Destruction is an important theme of human experience, and they don't get it from their education.

—**Camille Paglia**, *social critic, writer, and feminist*

Many successful people have compiled lists of qualities they consider essential for success. The bottom line on these lists is that one should be open-minded, have diverse interests, and be sensible.

1. Do not descend too deeply into specialism in your work. Educate all your parts. You will be healthier. Replace cynicism with its old-fashioned antidote, skepticism. Don't confuse success with excellence. The poet Robert Penn Warren, who taught at Yale for many years, once told me that "careerism is death."

2. Travel. Do not get stuck in one place. Visit Yellowstone or Yosemite or Appomattox, where our country really came together. Whatever you do, walk over the Brooklyn Bridge.

3. Listen to jazz music, the only art form Americans have ever invented, and a painless way, Wynton Marsalis reminds us, "of understanding ourselves."

4. Give up addictions. Try brushing your teeth tonight with the other hand.
—*Ken Burns,* documentary filmmaker

The era we live in belongs to people who believe in themselves, but are focused on the needs of others. And those people have three things in common:

1. They learn every day.

2. They have the courage to live their dreams.

3. They build trust in others.

By doing this, they lead a life that is fulfilling, interesting, and fun.
—*Jeffrey Immelt*, chairman
and CEO of General Electric

Six essential qualities that are the key to success:
1. Sincerity
2. Personal integrity
3. Humility
4. Courtesy
5. Wisdom
6. Charity
—*William Menninger,* psychiatrist

1. Never put off until tomorrow what you can do today.
2. Never trouble another for what you can do yourself.
3. Never spend your money before you have it.
4. Never buy what you do not want because it is cheap.

5. Pride costs us more than hunger, thirst, and cold.

6. We never repent of having eaten too little.

7. Nothing is troublesome that we do willingly.

8. How much pain has cost us the evils which never have happened.

9. Take things always by their smooth handle.

10. When angry, count ten, before you speak; if very angry, a hundred.

—*Thomas Jefferson*, U.S. president

Determination is ambition fueled by will. Do you have the determination to achieve your goals? If you do, you'll use everything at your disposal to succeed. This may include friends, family, and other people who will support you creatively, emotionally, or financially. You realize that if you really want to succeed at something, you'll make the time for it, take the risk for it, and do your best to ease any doubts about it. You'll do whatever it takes not to give up.

BEING DETERMINED

The secret of success is constancy to purpose.
—Benjamin Disraeli,
U.K. prime minister

*The way to learn to do things is to
do things. The way to learn a trade is to
work at it. Success teaches how
to succeed. Begin with the determination to
succeed, and the work is half done already.*
—Mark Twain, *writer, journalist,
and humorist*

KNOW THE VALUE OF PERSISTENCE

Stubborn persistence may be the critical factor that separates you from the competition. Scientist Thomas Edison, inventor of the lightbulb, phonograph, and 1,091 other revolutionary technologies, persisted through many failures because he knew how to "stick to it."

Sticking to it is the genius! Any other bright-minded fellow can accomplish just as much [as I did] if he will stick like hell and remember nothing that's any good works by itself. You got to make the damn thing work. I'll never give up, for I may have a streak of luck before I die.

—*Thomas Edison*, inventor

Obstacles cannot crush me. Every obstacle yields to stern resolve. He who is fixed to a star does not change his mind.

—*Leonardo da Vinci*, scientist, inventor, and artist

Failure or success seems to have been allotted to men by their stars. But they retain the power of wriggling, of fighting with their star or against it, and in the whole universe the only really interesting movement is this wriggle.

—*Edward Morgan (E.M.) Forster*, writer

Of course, persistence is related to passion. Scientist Koichi Tanaka describes the dogged determination it took to succeed at the experiment in laser-assisted soft ionization that won him the Nobel Prize in Chemistry.

> . . . Persistence is a must. I failed for weeks and months before I succeeded in making an ion. Why did I continue the experiment? Because I enjoyed it. It was fun for me to come to know something that I had never known before, and that fun enabled me to be persistent.
>
> —*Koichi Tanaka*, Nobel Prize winner
> in Chemistry

ⸯ

> Strong motivation is the most important factor in getting you to the top.
>
> —*Edmund Hillary*, mountaineer

Some goal-setters lose their will when they lose sight of their ultimate goal. Don't let the details block your view.

> If someone is struggling with their first book, the only advice I would give them is "Just get to the end, then worry. But do finish it." Then you'll know what you have in front of you. Don't worry about the little decisions along the way.
>
> —*Martin Amis*, writer

FIND SOMEONE TO EMULATE

For figure skater Scott Hamilton, his sense of self and the inspiration for his success was his mother, who struggled to pay for his lessons while she fought cancer.

∽

If you believe in the spirituality of a life force that is constant and forever, I think I absorbed a lot of her strength and a lot of her passion to hold it together and to fight through whatever obstacles lay in front of me. I always admired her strength and I always admired her courage. Without strength and courage it's really hard to perform at the highest levels of international figure skating, because you're alone on the ice and you only have seven minutes over two nights to prove yourself. And if you make any mistakes, you're dead. So I really feel like a lot of the qualities my mother had, and a lot of what she showed us with passed away. It gave me what I needed to be successful in figure skating.

—**Scott Hamilton**, *figure skater*

∽

It may help to have someone to look up to—at least to assure you that your goals are indeed attainable. Actor Jim Carrey's role model was comedian Rodney Dangerfield.

> He [Dangerfield] struggled for decades before he reached the top of his profession. I don't know if anybody remembers the era of the comedy club— they were quite popular places at one time, you can only see them now in the Smithsonian, I think—but I did stand-up in clubs for fifteen years and sometimes the only thing that kept me going was the thought that Rodney had dropped out of the business when he was thirty but had come back and made it big when he was in his forties. Made it big. In a business that almost always values youth over talent, he was—and still is—absolute proof that it's never too late to make your mark. You may have to quit for a while and sell some aluminum siding, but you don't have to give up your dreams.
>
> —*Jim Carrey*, actor and comedian

DISREGARD WHAT
PEOPLE SAY ABOUT AGE

Some people foolishly give up—or never start—to follow their ambitions because they believe that big goals are only for the young.

. . . Recognize that life doesn't end at thirty. If you don't hit the ball at an early age there is still plenty of time to do it. As Yogi Berra said, 'It's not [sic] over till it's over.' The classic example of that is Ray Kroc, who didn't really get involved with McDonald's until his late fifties. He was a salesperson for milk shake machines until then and people wouldn't say that he was successful. He was always striving but hadn't really had a great success, and then in California he came upon the McDonald brothers who had a hamburger stand and he saw that they were getting a lot of people through this facility, and he said, "By gosh, if I can persuade them to open more facilities, I can sell them more milk shake machines." But the McDonald brothers didn't have much ambition, which Ray Kroc did, so he bought them out, and the rest, as they say, is history. So there is a man who didn't really come into his own until when many people are thinking of retirement.

—*Malcolm Stevenson (Steve) Forbes*, president, CEO, and editor-in-chief of *Forbes*

FIGHT FRUSTRATION WITH OPTIMISM

Optimism, warranted or not, will help you when you're frustrated and the odds are against you. Some call such optimism a belief in miracles.

I'm the person in the lifeboat, where if the lifeboat was full of holes and going down and all there was was a Dixie cup, I'd be the one still bailing the water even though clearly that Dixie cup would not be able to get the water out in time to save the boat. But I would be of this belief that it could happen. Maybe I've just had too many experiences in my life where I've had things which were not supposed to happen to me: none of this was ever supposed to happen to me, I was never supposed to have a film career, and I didn't go to film school.

—*Michael Moore,* writer, filmmaker, and political activist

∽

No pessimist ever discovered the secrets of the stars, or sailed to an uncharted land, or opened a new heaven to the human spirit.

—*Helen Keller,* author and activist

FIND SOMEONE TO SUPPORT YOU

Reaching a goal is easier when you have someone else who believes in you. Ideally, that person will support you when times are tough. He or she will remind you of your objective and be determined for you when you're losing steam.

Writer Stephen King has his wife, Tabitha. In his acceptance speech for the National Book Award, he said:

> There were some hard, dark years before *Carrie*. We had two kids and no money. We rotated the bills, paying on different ones each month. I kept our car, an old Buick, going with duct tape and bailing wire. It was a time when my wife might have been expected to say, "Why don't you quit spending three hours a night in the laundry room, Steve, smoking cigarettes and drinking beer we can't afford? Why don't you get an actual job?"
>
> —*Stephen King*, writer

ॐ

> The dream begins with a teacher who believes in you, who tugs and pushes and leads you to the next plateau, sometimes poking you with a sharp stick called "truth."
>
> —*Dan Rather*, news anchor

ANCHOR YOURSELF IN YOUR CAUSE

Some people have goals that have moral momentum; that is, they are struggling for a cause. Whether or not your goal is to change the world, let the power of your convictions and those of others fuel you.

I thought often during my years in the White House of an admonition that we received in our small school in Plains, Georgia, from a beloved teacher, Miss Julia Coleman. She often said: "We must adjust to changing times and still hold to unchanging principles." When I was a young boy, this same teacher also introduced me to Leo Tolstoy's novel, *War and Peace.* She interpreted that powerful narrative as a reminder that the simple human attributes of goodness and truth can overcome great power. She also taught us that an individual is not swept along on a tide of inevitability but can influence even the greatest human events.

—*Jimmy Carter,* U.S. president and Nobel Laureate (in his acceptance speech of the Nobel Peace Prize)

For writer Zora Neale Hurston, being determined means not giving up, even when the cards were stacked against her.

. . . It seems to me that if I say a whole system must be upset for me to win, I am saying that I cannot sit in the game, and that safer rules must be made to give me a chance. I repudiate that. If others are in there, deal me a hand and let me see what I can make of it, even though I know some in there are dealing from the bottom and cheating like hell in other ways. If I can win anything in a game like that, I know I'll end up with the pot if the sharks can be eliminated.

—*Zora Neale Hurston,* writer

For many people (but not all), success means rising to the top, which means outperforming others in a bid to win something. Your competition may push you to take an extra risk, to try a little harder than you would otherwise. Perhaps competitiveness is related to a survival instinct that tells you that resources are limited and you must struggle against others for them. Even if your take on success is not so Darwinian, you are still competing with yourself as you try to match or exceed your own expectations.

BEING COMPETITIVE

*As a final incentive before
giving up a difficult task, try to imagine
it successfully accomplished by
someone you violently dislike.*
—**K. Zenios**, *aphorist*

*How can a brain know whether there
is something worth striving for? Well, it can
look around and see how well-off
other people are. If they can achieve
something, maybe so can you. Other people
anchor your well-being scale and tell you
what you can reasonably hope to achieve.*
—**Steven Pinker**, *research psychologist*

ADAPT TO SURVIVE

Under intensely competitive conditions, you may find yourself taking risks that you otherwise wouldn't consider.

When we were number two in the ratings, when Jeff Zucker started as executive producer and I had just started as the anchor, I think that's when we did some of our best shows because we tried so many different things. We took so many risks. We would do really long segments or, you know, we'd be all over the place. We would do very unexpected things. And I just loved the show.

—*Katie Couric*, television host

The reason I went into the salad-dressing business is because I suddenly realized I needed a different power base. When Reagan became president, I discovered I had been end-played and that the power base I formerly operated from no longer existed. I realized that to be effective I would have to enter the world of business.

—*Paul Newman*, actor and businessperson

Use your competitiveness to motivate yourself.

The way to get things done is to stimulate competition. I do not mean in a sordid, money-getting way, but in the desire to excel.

—*Charles Schwab,* industrialist and financier

A useless mate I went to school with directed a commercial and got paid copious amounts of money for it. And the commercial was a pile of shit! The fact that he managed to get the job and that he had the balls to call himself a director was enough to inspire me—he was a director because he was making money. He was 24. I was 25, and I didn't have a job and that wasn't good because I knew it takes five years before you get anywhere in your job. So I was thinking, At this point I'll be 30 years old before I get anywhere. I began to panic. . . . I'd read that Steven Spielberg made his first movie when he was 26. So I wanted to shoot a narrative by the time I was 26. And somehow I did it; I made a short film called *Hard Case.*

—*Guy Ritchie,* director

Being competitive means making strategic decisions. To be competitive as an A-list actor, Chloë Sevigny must be selective about what films she agrees to appear in, yet she needs to make ends meet. Her compromise:

> . . . I've had to turn to doing commercial work like the H&M campaign. I hate myself for doing things like that, but it's the only way I can survive financially. I know it will be up on the telephone booths for however long, and then it will disappear. A film is there forever . . . If I came from a wealthy family and didn't need the money, then maybe I would have been able to refuse the offer, but I don't. It's me surviving the movie industry. I'd still rather do an ad than some romantic comedy that I would later hate myself for.
>
> —*Chloë Sevigny*, actor

Practiced in moderation, a "survival of the fittest" mentality can also help you sharpen your own skills.

> . . . In circumstances where survival is the key, any human characteristic or quality you can dredge up must be used. If you are strong physically, you use your strength; if you have charisma and inner dignity, you use them. If you have charm, you use charm . . .
>
> —*Stephen Fry*, writer, actor, and comedian

SET YOURSELF APART

How **can you beat the competition? For one, dare to be different from them.**

> One must change one's tactics every ten years if one wishes to maintain one's superiority.
> —*Napoleon Bonaparte*, general and emperor of France

Being the first to do something is the most obvious way to set yourself apart from others.

> As long ago as 150 B.C., the Roman playwright Terence said it best: "Do not do what is already done." You must be the first. Or the fastest. Or the most convenient. Or you must deliver more value for the money. In the U.S.: McDonald's was the first to popularize the concept of fast food.
>
> FedEx was the first to offer time-certain delivery.
>
> Sears & Roebuck was able to offer the convenience of catalog shopping.
>
> Dell Computers was the first to sell customized computers online.
>
> So it's the uniqueness of your idea that will attract the financial support to get things off the ground.
> —*Frederick Smith*, chairman, president, and CEO of FedEx

Approach a problem in a new way to set yourself apart from your competition. Michael Dell, founder of Dell computer, did this when he was a teenage newspaper salesperson for the *Houston Post*. Dell found a new way to sell thousands of new subscriptions:

> There were two kinds of people who almost always bought subscriptions to the *Post:* people who had just married and people who had just moved into new houses or apartments. With this in mind I wondered, "How could you find all the people who are getting mortgages or are getting married?" After asking around, I discovered that when a couple wanted to get married, they had to go to the county courthouse and get a marriage license. . . Then I found out that certain companies compiled lists of people who had applied for mortgages. These lists were ranked by the size of the mortgage. You could easily identify the people with the highest mortgages and go after those high-potential customers first. (This is my first experience with what I would later call "segmenting the market," one of Dell's most significant strategies for success.)
>
> —*Michael Dell,* founder and CEO of Dell

*The secret of success is to
know something nobody else knows.*

—**Aristotle Onassis**, shipping magnate

PLAY BY YOUR OWN RULES

Kofi Annan and Meryl Streep share a similar philosophy about how one should deal with competition. Annan describes how he dealt with the intense competition among his classmates at MIT:

> At the outset, there was competition—rather intense competition—among my cohorts. Each was equally determined to shine and to demonstrate his leadership abilities. I say 'his,' because there were no women among us; I am certainly glad that has changed. Walking along the Charles River one day, in the middle of my first term, I reflected on my predicament. How could I survive, let alone thrive, in this group of overachievers? And the answer came to me most emphatically: NOT by playing it according to their rules. 'Follow your own inner compass,' I said to myself, 'listen to your own drummer.' To live is to choose. But to choose well, you must know who you are, what you stand for, where you want to go and why you want to get there. My anxieties slowly began to dissolve.
>
> —*Kofi Annan*, secretary-general of the United Nations

Success is often provided by the exception to the Rules for Success. People who have broken through color and gender lines, class and cultural bias, have done so despite an array of reasons as to why they shouldn't be able to do so. In this way, success may ultimately have more to do with your own personality, focus, and optimism than your gender, race or background. Put blinders on to those things that conspire to hold you back, especially the ones in your own head. Guard your good mood. Listen to music every day, joke, and love and read more for fun, especially poetry.

—*Meryl Streep,* actor

In a classic case of making your own rules, boxer George Foreman ignored the warnings others, including a daughter, gave him when he announced his decision to return to boxing at an advanced age. Needless to say, he won the fight.

Don't have that conversation with yourself where you say, 'He's got more talent than I do,' or 'She's faster than I am.' Success depends on what's in your mind. I can tell you then being a boxing champion means more than physically waking up one morning and discovering a muscle or two. It happens from the tip of your toes all the way up to the crown of your head. Success is about your spirit. . . .

—*George Foreman,* heavyweight boxing champion and entrepreneur

MARKET YOURSELF

Your work may be no better than that of your competition. The difference might come in how to present your work or your idea to appeal to the people to whom you're selling it. It's called self-promotion.

Only those artists who have an ability in marketing can survive in the art world. Damien Hirst is a good example. Through his art, you can see the process of how an artist can survive in the art world. First of all, distinctively situate his/her position in art history. Second, articulate what the beauty of his/her art is. Next, sexuality. Then, death. Present what he/she finds in death. If an artist aptly rotates this cycle, he/she can survive. Damien Hirst has been repeating the cycle of birth, death, love, sex, and beauty.

—*Takashi Murakami,* artist

In the modern world of business, it is useless to be a creative, original thinker unless you can also sell what you create.

—*David Ogilvy,* founder of Ogilvy & Mather

COMPETE WITH
YOURSELF MOST OF ALL

If you focus too much on your competition, you might lose sight of your real goals.

I think when you become too obsessed with those ratings you really lose sight of your job, which is to put on a great show that you really love and that you think is entertaining and informative and enlightening.

—*Katie Couric,* television host

Beware: extreme competitiveness can make one misanthropic and egotistical.

It interests me because the national culture is founded very much on the idea of strive and succeed. Instead of rising with the masses one should rise from the masses. Your extremity is my opportunity. That's what forms the basis of our economic life, and this is what forms the rest of our lives. That American myth: the idea of something out of nothing. And this also affects the spirit of the individual. It's very divisive. One feels one can only succeed at the cost of someone else.

—*David Mamet,* playwright

The most important point about competition is that it gives you a framework in which to accomplish new things. The emphasis isn't on another person's accomplishments; it's on yours. If you can outdo yourself, you'll succeed no matter what. The cocreator of the Apple Macintosh computer understood this.

People don't understand, for the most part, the idea of competing with yourself. If you can do something better, put it out alongside what you presently have and let natural selection take care of it. You win in either case. If your old product remains popular, you win. If your new product takes off, you win. This was the argument I used at Apple. I was told, 'We can't possibly produce the Macintosh. It doesn't have Apple II compatibility.'

—*Jef Raskin,* cocreator of the Macintosh interface

Whether your goal is to be

an artist, entrepreneur, CEO, politician, Nobel Prize winner, or something else, there's a pretty good chance you'll interact with other people along the way. Unless your plan is to work in a vacuum and be unknown to anyone ever, you'll have to factor these other people into your equation of success—partners, patrons, investors, bosses, colleagues, clients, constituents, customers, and/or critics. Depending on your goal, working with others may be a big factor or a little factor, but it almost certainly counts.

WORKING WITH
OTHERS

Be civil to all; sociable to many;
familiar with few; friend to one;
enemy to none.
—Benjamin Franklin,
statesman and inventor

REALIZE THAT YOU NEED OTHERS

No matter how independent we are as individuals, we depend upon others to define ourselves and create purpose in our lives.

Coming together is a beginning; keeping together is progress; working together is success.

—**Henry Ford,** founder of the Ford Motor Company

There is no such thing as a 'self-made' man. We are made up of thousands of others. Everyone who has ever done a kind deed for us, or spoken one word of encouragement to us, has entered into the makeup of our character and of our thoughts, as well as our success.

—**George Adams,** *musician*

All lives are a struggle against selfishness. All my life I've stood a little apart from institutions I willingly joined. It just felt natural to me. But if my life had shared no common purpose, it wouldn't have amounted to much beyond eccentricity. There is no honor or happiness in just being strong enough to be left alone.

—**John McCain,** U.S. senator

GET THEM TO IDENTIFY WITH YOU

Finding out *how* successful people get others to work with them or for them is always interesting. The bottom line is that you need to make an effort to identify with others and to get others to identify with you.

You would laugh if you knew all I learned in order to talk to clients who were mostly men. I learned to talk horses with Jack Landry at Philip Morris, who had a lot to do with the Marlboro Cup race that Philip Morris sponsored; he thought it was hilarious that I knew anything about horses, but horse talk helped forge our friendship. Once I had a client who was a big elk hunter and he always looked into the eyes of the men at the lunch table, not into mine, when he talked elks. I didn't know what an elk was, so I went to the library and found out all about elks and elk hunting. It didn't take me long to learn more about elks than anybody else on Madison Avenue, and he started looking into my eyes when he talked about his elks. I learned about African big-game hunting and salmon fishing. I was an expert on government regulations from A to Z and that was a hit with every client I ever had. I learned about California wines, antique cars, Swiss cantons, mountain walking boots, what makes a good suit, rare fish, western six-guns, the Boy Scouts, the best hotels, and where he could take his kids to have fun in almost every city in the Western world.

—**Mary Wells Lawrence**, founder and CEO of Wells Rich Greene

I don't have any pretense of intellectual superiority. I'm a smart person who's sort of a regular guy, who asks good questions that people would ask themselves, if they had the opportunity to be in my shoes.

—**Larry King**, talk show host

. . . One of the many aspects of *60 Minutes's* success—its genius, even—is how accessible those five reporters are, how intimately they communicate with their viewers. There's a lesson there for all of us . . . One of the strengths of *60 Minutes* is that the people on the screen seem real, probably because they ARE. When Ed Bradley or Lesley Stahl leans forward and asks the tough question we're all dying to ask, their passion and curiosity are genuine; Ed or Lesley would tell you the same story exactly the same way in the newsroom or in the bar downstairs.

—**Andrew Heyward**, president of CBS News

. . . I like to believe that I try to make things simple to understand. And frankly, if I can understand it, then I figure everybody else can understand it. . . But I try to make things [as] simple and clear as I can, and I think that helps you persuade other people.

—**Jack Valenti,** *former president and CEO of the Motion Picture Association of America*

DON'T WORRY SO MUCH ABOUT GETTING CREDIT

You may need to work with others as partners or in teams, or working under another person or within a corporation. Helen Gurley Brown's superior understanding of social organizations facilitated her rise from secretary to publishing dynamo.

Wherever you are on the success ladder, you probably still have a boss and probably will unless you go into business for yourself; even presidents and chairmen of corporations have bosses (boards of directors). Your job, always, is to make that person above you look good at the same time that you get what *you* need from the job. You try to 'lighten the load' for him or her—and I'm not just talking about assistants and secretaries lightening the load, but about executives working for other executives. Actually, the better job you do, the better it is for the person above you. Don't worry about the boss getting credit for what you do. He or she usually will, but that isn't as bad as it sounds. People who are good are good, and though the boss may not give you public credit, the word gets around.

—*Helen Gurley Brown,* editor-in-chief of Cosmopolitan international editions

GET THE RESPECT OF OTHERS

Respect is a strong motivator of success.

Mark Twain, at the end of a profoundly meaningful life, for which he never received a Nobel Prize, asked himself what it was we all lived for. He came up with six words which satisfied him. They satisfy me, too. They should satisfy you. *'The good opinion of our neighbors.'*
—***Kurt Vonnegut***, writer

There is only one rule of success that really counts in the long run. Success is measured by how many people on this earth *respect* you. . . .But this is not an easy standard. It's not easy to achieve the kind of success and respect I'm talking about. It requires a consistency of behavior that is truly *impressive*. It requires that you treat others in an honest and caring way. When someone else feels that you are not fair, or that you are putting your welfare ahead of his, you will not be respected. . . . The first step to gaining respect is pretty difficult: *Always do what you say you are going to do.*
—***Bill O'Reilly***, news show host

If you're like some self-conscious achievers, your success may be spurred on by the fear that others will disrespect you if you don't do your best.

I guess I have a very low threshold of embarrassment. And I just don't like embarrassing myself. You know we have this—the theatre and the machinery and the people—and every day we try to put on a new show . . . and it all comes down to the one hour, 5:30 to 6:30. If I somehow do something stupid that embarrasses me, I feel like I've thrown away that effort for the day. It's very frustrating. But I think it's the same for anybody, you know, regardless of your work. It's like a baseball player: a big game, and an important series, a pennant race and you go o for 4—I mean that's embarrassing. That guy goes into the dugout and takes the bat to the water cooler. It's the same thing. I think humans just don't want to embarrass themselves.

—*David Letterman,* talk show host

WATCH YOUR WORDS

To successful people, working with others means knowing what to say—*and* what not to say. This observation has inspired a number of pithy quotes.

Abrasive personality is the single most frequent cause for failure of bright men and women in the executive ranks of business and industry.
—**Harry Levinson,** psychologist

Remember not only to say the right thing in the right place, but far more difficult still, to leave unsaid the wrong thing at the tempting moment.
—**Benjamin Franklin**, statesman and inventor

To be a social success, do not act pathetic, arrogant, or bored. Do not discuss your unhappy childhood, your visit to the dentist, the shortcomings of your cleaning woman, the state of your bowels, or your spouse's bad habits.
—**Mason Cooley**, aphorist

The secret of success is sincerity. Once you can fake that you've got it made.
—**Daniel Schorr,** journalist

If A is a success in life,
then A equals x plus y plus z.
Work is x; y is play;
and z is keeping your mouth shut.

—**Albert Einstein**, *physicist*

HANDLE DIFFICULT PEOPLE WITH CARE

Some jobs require better social skills than others. From those who must constantly interact with others, there's a good chance you'll encounter difficult people. Here are a few suggestions for successfully dealing with them.

❧

Sometimes people say unkind or thoughtless things, and when they do, it is best to be a little hard of hearing—to tune out and not snap back in anger or impatience. Anger, resentment, envy, and self-pity are wasteful reactions. They greatly drain one's time. They sap energy better devoted to productive endeavors. Of course it is important to be a good listener—to pay attention to teachers, coworkers, and spouses. But is also pays, sometimes, to be a little deaf.

—**Ruth Bader Ginsburg**, U.S. Supreme Court justice

❧

Always write angry letters to your enemies. Never mail them. This way you get the anger out of your system while minimizing the amount of your time that is controlled by those you dislike. . . . Disbelieve both the best and the worst that others say about you. Realize that whatever you say about people will inevitably get back to them.

—*James Fallows,* journalist

. . . A lot of problems with interpersonal relationships, whether they are friendships, romance, or professional relationships is that frequently difficulties are rooted in unexpressed expectations. When someone has expectations of you, you disappoint them even when they are not expressed. They become unexpressed and unmet expectations. So often in life, that happens. What happens if you say, "I never knew that, I never knew you expected that of me. You never expressed it." They say, "Well, I thought it. I thought it was obvious." For whatever it may be worth, the longer I go, the more I know that unexpressed and unmet expectations are a great taproot of difficulty in interpersonal relationships.

—*Dan Rather,* news anchor

HAVE A HEALTHY SKEPTICISM
OF AUTHORITY

The famous physicist Richard Feynman argued that a skeptical mind is as necessary for success in the world of politics and people as it is in the world of science. Question the people who tell you what to do and think.

One of the things that my father taught me besides physics, whether it's correct or not, was a disrespect for the respectable . . . 'Here is one human standing here and the others are bowing. Now what is the difference? This one is the Pope'. . . . 'But this man has the same human problems, he eats dinner like anybody else, he goes to the bathroom, he has the same kind of problems as everybody, he's a human being. Why are they all bowing to him? Only because of his name and his position, because of his uniform, not because of something special he did, or his honor, or something like that.'

—*Richard Feynman,* Nobel Prize winner
in Physics

❧

If it's a good idea, go ahead and do it. It is much easier to apologize than it is to get permission.

—*Grace Hopper,* admiral

❧

The fastest way to succeed is to look as if you're playing by somebody else's rules, while quietly playing by your own.

—*Michael Korda*, publisher

∽

"Do not believe in anything simply because you have heard it. Do not believe in anything simply because it is spoken and rumored by many. Do not believe in anything simply because it is found written in your religious books. Do not believe in anything merely on the authority of your teachers and elders. Do not believe in traditions because they have been handed down for many generations. But after observation and analysis, when you find that anything agrees with reason and is conducive to the good and benefit of one and all, then accept it and live up to it."

—*Prince Gautama Siddharta* (Buddha)

DON'T BE AFRAID
TO DEPEND ON OTHERS

Don't be afraid to ask for help; your success might depend on it.

✑

There is magic that results when a person invests in you. He becomes a big-time investor in your success, a stockholder in your dreams. Because, when you ask someone for help, you are implicitly asking him to place a bet on you. The more people you get to bet on you, the larger your network of investors and the shorter the odds.

This isn't Pollyanna I'm talking. It comes from the smartest man who ever wrote about politics, or human nature for that matter, Niccolò Machiavelli. "Men are by nature as much bound by the benefits they confer as by those they receive." "If you want to make a friend," said Benjamin Franklin, a fellow who grows wiser the older I get, "let someone do you a favor."

—**Christopher Matthews**, *journalist and talk show host*

✑

But what do you do if your success depends upon the performance of a partner or colleague? On his partnership with Dr. James Watson that resulted in the discovery of DNA, Francis Crick wrote:

> . . . You have to be on such candid terms that when the other produces an idea you can criticize it very freely without being offensive and so on. So that means that if one of you gets an idea which is [a] cul-de-sac, which gets you in off on a false trail, the other one will pull you back and get you out of it. And I think that's really what helped. That every time one of us had a false idea the other would be very critical about it. And there are a number of cases of that we can actually document.
>
> —*Francis Crick*, molecular biologist and codiscover of the structure of DNA

On his partnership with president and COO Ken Rollins, Michael Dell, CEO of Dell Computers, said:

> I'm concerned about, "What do we have to get done to be successful?" There's way too much to get done to have a proprietary interest in who's going to do it, or even worse, who's going to get credit for it.
>
> —*Michael Dell*, CEO of Dell Computers

When asked to define the secret of their success in a word or two, most people say "hard work." No matter how passionate you are about your work, it may test your stamina and resolve. But what does hard work mean? What energies are required to stay the course? How does one know what to work hard at? These questions are addressed elsewhere in this book. This chapter is simply a tribute to the virtues of mulish, dogged, driven, near-obsessive, long-term dedication to a vision or a task at hand.

WORKING HARD

❧

*No one can arrive from
being talented alone. God gives talent;
work transforms talent into genius.*
—**Anna Pavlova, poet**

❧

*Some people dream of success
. . . while others wake up and work
hard at it.*
—**Anonymous**

❧

UNDERSTAND THE
VALUE OF HARD WORK

From Abraham Lincoln to Larry Bird, every successful person has issued one-liners about how hard work made them successful.

A winner is someone who recognizes his God-given talents, works his tail off to develop them into skills, and uses these skills to accomplish his goals.
—*Larry Bird*, basketball player

People of mediocre ability sometimes achieve outstanding success because they don't know when to quit.
—*George Allen*, U.S. senator

Things may come to those who wait. But only the things left by those who hustle.
—*Abraham Lincoln*, U.S. president

Success usually comes to those who are too busy to be looking for it.
—*Henry David Thoreau,* writer, philosopher, and naturalist

*I know the price of success:
dedication, hard work,
and an unremitting devotion to
the things you want to see happen.*

—**Frank Lloyd Wright**, architect

DETERMINE WHAT SACRIFICES YOU'RE WILLING TO MAKE

Hard work requires uncommon discipline. Ask yourself if you're willing to do it, and to what extent. Would you be willing to endure what writer Philip K. Dick endured?

I used to just get up at noon and sit down at the typewriter and write until 2 A.M. Just write from noon in the morning until 2 A.M. You've got to do that when you start out. Or you're going to die on the vine. I mean you've got to just—you're going to live on two thousand dollars a year. You're going to eat rocks and dirt and weeds from the back yard for the first ten years. And then after the first ten years, you get to eat instant breakfast. You work up till you're rich enough to get a phone put in. And you get to buy an old automobile. And you get to drive around in an old automobile, which you crank-start every morning. And then after 25 years, you manage to get a used Dodge. It costs you $795.00, but, the radio doesn't work in it. And there's people that're standing behind grocery counters and are making more money.

—*Philip K. Dick,* writer

My life in wrestling is one-eighth talent and seven-eighths discipline. I believe that my life as a writer consists of one-eighth talent and seven-eighths discipline, too.

—*John Irving*, writer

Hard work may pay off after all despite the cliché, "no one on their deathbed ever said, 'I wish I spent more time at the office.'"

No man on his deathbed ever said, "I wish I had spent more time at the office." How does he know that? I'll bet someone on their deathbed said, "I wish I had spent more time at the office in my twenties and thirties, I would have had a much better life"—gurgle—dead.

—*Al Franken*, comedian and political commentator

Shakespeare wrote his sonnets within a strict discipline, fourteen lines of iambic pentameter, rhyming in three quatrains and a couplet. Were his sonnets dull? Mozart wrote his sonatas within an equally rigid discipline—exposition, development, and recapitulation. Were they dull?

—*David Ogilvy*, founder of Ogilvy & Mather

For successful people like Madeleine Albright, the act of working hard, of continuously striving toward something, is a reward in itself.

◌

I have always believed, because I learned it from my parents, that you have to fight to achieve all you can, not literally but with the gifts you have. At first to me that meant doing well in school. Later it meant being a good wife and mother and so on through all the stages of my life up to and including Secretary of State and beyond. I was taught to strive not because there were any guarantees of success but because the act of striving is in itself the only way to keep faith with life.

—Madeleine Albright,
former U.S. Secretary of State

◌

Always remember that striving and struggle precede success, even in the dictionary.

—Sarah Ban Breathnach, writer

HAVE A REGIMEN

Hard work is harder without some semblance of structure. Establish a routine. For writers such as Roald Dahl, the work routine is brief but intense.

My work routine is very simple and it's always been so for the last 45 years. The great thing, of course, is never to work too long at a stretch, because after two hours you are not at your highest peak of concentration, so you have to stop. . . . I start at 10 o'clock and I stop at 12. Always. However well I'm going, I will stay there until 12, even if I'm a bit stuck. You have to keep your bottom on the chair and stick it out. Otherwise, if you start getting in the habit of walking away, you'll never get it done.

—*Roald Dahl,* writer

❧

Be regular and orderly in your life, that you may be violent and original in your work.

—*Clive Barker,* writer

❧

I go to my studio everyday. Some days the work comes easily. Other days nothing happens. Yet on the good days the inspiration is only an accumulation of all the other days, the nonproductive ones.

—*Beverly Pepper,* artist

STEP BACK EVERY ONCE IN A WHILE

But take a step back if you begin to feel that your hard work ceases to be meaningful.

Every now and then go away, have a little relaxation, for when you come back to your work your judgment will be surer since to remain constantly at work will cause you to lose power of judgment. Go some distance away because then the work appears smaller, and more of it can be taken in at a glance, and a lack of harmony or portion is more readily seen.

—*Leonardo da Vinci,* scientist, inventor, and artist

Success isn't always an individual achievement. In fact, it often isn't. Your success may depend upon countless others, especially the people who support you in your day-to-day work. Good leadership skills aren't essential for every career path. Poets and painters don't need them as much as CEOs, teachers, or activists. Regardless, knowing how to lead others to see and share your vision will only help you to achieve it.

LEADING OTHERS

❧

*The leadership instinct you are born with
is the backbone. You develop the funny
bone and the wishbone that go with it.*
—Elaine Agather, *chairman and CEO
of JPMorgan Chase—Dallas*

❧

*Leadership is a potent combination
of strategy and character. But if you must
be without one, be without the strategy.*
—H. Norman Schwarzkopf, *general*

❧

*Ninety percent of leadership is the ability
to communicate something people want.*
—Dianne Feinstein, *U.S. senator*

❧

PICK THE RIGHT PEOPLE
TO WORK WITH YOU

Mountaineer Edmund Hillary has suggestions for selecting the perfect group on an expedition. His criteria may also be applied to situations in which your life isn't *literally* in the hands of your team.

If I'm selecting a group, the first thing one has to look for is a record of achievement. It may be modest achievement, but people have shown that they can persist, they can carry out objectives and get to a final solution. If they can do that on small things, there's a very good chance that they'll perform well on big things at the same time. And I'm a great believer in a really good sense of humor. If you have someone in an expedition who's reasonably competent and has a great sense of humor, they're a very stimulating factor for the whole team, and they play a very important psychological part in the success of the team.

—*Edmund Hillary,* mountaineer

Make sure to express your appreciation. It doesn't take much effort for you and it may mean a lot to them.

Appreciate everything your associates do for the business. Nothing else can quite substitute for a few well-chosen, well-timed, sincere words of praise. They're absolutely free and worth a fortune.

—*Sam Walton,* cofounder of Wal-Mart

FOSTER TRUST AND OPENNESS

Be straightforward with the people who work for you. Keep doors and minds open. Communicate with your colleagues. Be open with them; it's a sign of respect, and all people want to be respected. If you do, they will be more inclined to support you through good and bad times.

A leader's greatest obligation is to make possible an environment where people's minds and hearts can be inventive, brave, human, and strong, where people can aspire to do useful and significant things, where people can aspire to change the world . . . At Hewlett-Packard we call this way of thinking, this set of behaviors, the rules of the garage . . . And our rules are, believe you can change the world, work quickly, keep the tools unlocked, work whenever, know when to work alone and when to work together; share tools, ideas, trust your colleagues. No politics, no bureaucracy: these are ridiculous in a garage. The customer defines a job well done. Radical ideas are not bad ideas. Invent different ways of working. Make a contribution every day. If it doesn't contribute, it doesn't leave the garage. Believe that together we can do anything. Invent.

—*Carleton (Carly) Fiorina,* former CEO of Hewlett-Packard

&c/o

People want to trust. They are hungry for it. But they are selective. They will only give it to a motivator—a communicator—a teacher—a real person—someone who, over time and across events, proves to be exactly what they say they are—someone who makes the commitments they can keep—and keeps the commitments they make.

To earn trust you must have values. Values are about personal consistency. Values give you a rock solid sense of who you are—what you believe in—which side you're on.
—*Jeffrey Immelt,* chairman and
CEO of General Electric

A biochemist working in the laboratory of Nobel Prize winner Paul Zamecnik describes the context in which they made their crucial discovery in protein synthesis.

[Nobel Prize winner Paul Zamecnik] created a laboratory atmosphere that was very informal, very relaxed, very good fun and very little pressure of competition in the laboratory. He also was strikingly generous in attributing, in recognizing the contributions of other people to the areas that he was working with, and urged his associates to be generous in their acknowledgment of the work of other people. I think this whole attitude contributed significantly to an openness and a sharing, which in turn contributed to the success of the laboratory.

—*Mahlon Hoagland,* biochemist

Solicit feedback from the people who work for you. See page 181 on getting feedback for more on this topic.

❦

. . . Before you take a position or make a decision, gather information and different perspectives. Don't be afraid to ask questions or say you don't know. Run meetings in a way in which you ask each person to offer his or her point of view. Try to get everyone to think about and articulate the advantages and disadvantages of a course of action.

—*Christie Hefner, Chairman and CEO of Playboy Enterprises*

❦

GET OTHERS TO TAKE OWNERSHIP

If you inspire the people working for you, they will be more inclined to be accountable for the work they do for you. An employee who takes ownership of a project is emotionally invested in it.

> Never tell people how to do things. Tell them what to do and they will surprise you with their ingenuity.
> —*General George S. Patton, Jr.,* general in the U.S. Army

∽

> Leadership is the art of getting someone else to do something you want done because he wants to do it.
> —*Dwight Eisenhower,* U.S. president

"Open source" is of the most popular paradigms in project management. You plant the seed for a project and invite others to share in its development and eventual success. It is an approach that is adopted from a popular method of software creation in which many people contribute to a project outside the confines of a rigid hierarchy.

> The way the leadership has evolved, and will continue to evolve, is that others handle other issues—to the point where I'm already just one of many. I'm just the most visible one, and the one whose decisions most people tend to respect.
> —*Linus Torvalds,* founder of Linux

USE HUMOR

Last but not least, never underestimate the power of levity in leadership. Jello Biafra and Al Franken both use humor and surprise to lead others effectively.

The value of shock is to stir the sediment in the brain, and wake people up. All my different kinds of artwork have been designed to inspire people to think. They may not always agree with me, but at least they will have some feelings and some passion about whatever it is I'm bombarding them with at the moment. I also think there's plenty of room, even in the most serious activist circles, for humor. Humor can be very effective both to inspire, and as a weapon. Just ask Frank Zappa and Charlie Chaplin.

—*Jello Biafra,* musician and political activist

I think that being able to make people laugh and write a book that's funny makes the information go down a lot easier and it makes it a lot more fun to read, easier to understand, and often stronger.

—*Al Franken,* comedian and political commentator

BE FIRM WHEN NECESSARY

Of course, when the time comes to make a decision there might not be a consensus. Or you may not have a choice but to make an unpopular move. Al Dunlap, aka "Chainsaw Al," was known for his tough guy reputation. His critics, however, say he went much too far in his ruthless attempts to downsize corporations to make them more profitable.

I think because in consensus you're mitigating to less than the best decision. Everyone has something to say. I think what you have to do, you have to listen to what everyone has to say, but then you've got to make a decision, and that's called leadership. Someone has to stand up and be accountable for the final decision.

—*Albert (Al) Dunlap*, former chairman and CEO of Sunbeam

The art of leadership is saying no, not yes. It is very easy to say yes.

—*Tony Blair*, prime minister of Great Britain

A truism: No risk, no reward. It's no shock that the most successful people seem to be those who take significant risks. They jeopardize their personal comfort. They challenge the status quo. They put their money and time at stake. Taking a risk is a creative act. It may mean approaching a task or situation in a completely different way or even stirring up trouble.

TAKING RISKS

❧

*There is nothing more difficult and
dangerous, or more doubtful of success, than
an attempt to introduce a new order
of things in any state. For the innovator has
for enemies all those who derived
advantages from the old order of things
while those who expect to be benefited by
the new institutions will be but
lukewarm defenders.*
—**Niccolò Machiavelli**, *political philosopher
and writer, in* The Prince

❧

*. . . Remember that the fear of failure is the
most paralyzing of all human
emotions. The fear of failure stops us from
trying, from daring, from succeeding.
It must be confronted. Don't grow
old saying, "I wish I had. I should have.
Why didn't I?" Failure is not to be dreaded,
but to confront, reject, and overcome.*
—**Mark Shields**, *journalist and
political commentator*

❧

SEE YOURSELF AS A RISK-TAKER

What are the characteristics of a risk-taker?

∽

. . . The crazy ones, the misfits, the rebels, the troublemakers. The round pegs in the square holes. The ones who see things differently. They're not fond of rules and they have no respect for the status quo. You can quote them, disagree with them, glorify or vilify them. About the only thing you can't do is ignore them, because they change things. They push the human race forward. And while some may see them as the crazy ones, we see genius. Because the people who are crazy enough to think they can change the world are the ones who do.

—Apple Computer, Inc.

∽

Risk-takers often ward off skepticism. One risk-taker who reaped reward is Nolan Bushnell, the founder of Atari. Skeptics were unconvinced with Bushnell's vision that games would drive the development of multimedia.

> . . . You'd go to these conferences, and they're called multimedia conferences. And they'd say, "What's the killer app?" And I'd say: "Guys, the killer app

for multimedia is games . . ." And then they'd say: "But what's *really* going to be important?" . . . People would look at you like you like you had three heads. "You mean you're going to put the TV set in a box with a coin slot and play games on it? Oh, and then you're going to have people hook them up to their own TV set? Oh, I don't think so."
—**Nolan Bushnell,** founder of Atari, Inc.

Fundamental progress has to do with the reinterpretation of basic ideas.
—**Alfred North Whitehead**, mathematician and philosopher

Wherever you see a successful business, someone once made a courageous decision.
—**Peter Drucker,** management consultant

On June 6th, 1944 thousands of American paratroopers jumped into Normandy. Four men refused the jump. Can you imagine, can anyone imagine the rest of these men's lives? What prodigies of self-excuse, rationale, or repression they must have had to employ? Their lives, in effect, ended the moment they refused to leave the plane. As would the lives of the Jews, had they refused to go into the sea. As will yours and mine, and as they do in part, we each refuse the opportunity to change—we stagnate and perform ever greater prodigies of repression and hypocrisy, to explain to ourselves why we don't immerse ourselves in the mysteries of life. We all die in the end, but there's no reason to die in the middle.

—**David Mamet**, *playwright*

MAKE NECESSITY AN ASSET

Risk-taking, like invention, is often born out of necessity. Take actor Tom Arnold, whose show business career started when he needed to pay his tuition.

. . . I'm broke and tuition is due, so I came up with my first legitimate scam. I'd walk twenty-one miles in my underwear, in the middle of winter, and people could pledge money. I wasn't curing cancer, but I needed some schoolin'. It was an incredibly stupid idea, so of course it caught on like wildfire. Before I knew it, the whole town was involved and I had $3,000. Then reporters from all over the country were calling. I was in the *New York Times* and the *National Enquirer*! Show business!

—**Tom Arnold**, writer, producer, and actor

Progress is what happens when impossibility yields to necessity.

—**Arnold Glasgow,** psychologist

BE UNCONVENTIONAL

Risk-takers dare to approach a situation in unconventional ways:

> No one can possibly achieve any real and lasting success or "get rich" in business by being a conformist.
> —*John Paul Getty*, founder of Getty Oil Company

> . . . I think the only rule is that when you finish something, you should look at it and ask, will this knock everybody on their ass?
> —*George Lois,* advertising executive

Being unconventional involves flexibility and an open mind. You'll need to be able to make unscripted decisions. If you're like Michael Moore, they will pay off.

> I don't start out with a script or a hard and fast outline of what we've got to shoot. I have an idea but a lot of times, I'll start out and . . . I get this idea: "Let's go to Canada and show how they've got so few guns and that's why they have so few murders." And you get there and you find out they've got a lot of guns. Well, okay. I like that. I like being fooled by my own thoughts and being challenged and being found wrong. And I feel that if I let you in on that journey, you'll be as surprised as I am.
> —*Michael Moore,* filmmaker and political activist

Director and producer James Brooks describes the experience of succeeding with the award-winning film, *As Good as It Gets*. The movie was a risky venture because it stars a misanthropic character that audiences hate at the beginning of the film. This unconventional movie was nominated for Best Picture at the Academy Awards (and its stars, Jack Nicholson and Helen Hunt, won Best Actor and Best Actress).

✑

Well, it's very hard to get the license to do something that doesn't fit into a cookie-cutter kind of formula. It's so hard to get the backing and the money to go out there where it is odd and curious, and where you don't quite know how to do it yourself. And the great thing is, we got the license to do it this time. It feels amazing now, because we were so scared it wouldn't work. This was a romantic comedy that didn't insist that you root for the couple to make it. I think that's what set it apart.

—**James Brooks**, *writer, producer, and director*

CALCULATE YOUR RISKS

For some risk-takers, the risks are always calculated. On winning the D.W. Griffith Award, film director Stanley Kubrick wrote about the legendary filmmaker for whom the award is named.

. . . Griffith was always ready to take tremendous risks in his films and in his business affairs. He was always ready to fly too high. And in the end, the wings of fortune proved, for him, like those of Icarus, to be made of nothing more substantial than wax and feathers. And like Icarus, when he flew too close to the sun, they melted, and the man whose fame exceeded the most illustrious filmmakers of today, spent the last 17 years of his life shunned by the film industry he had created.

I've compared Griffith's career to the Icarus myth, but at the same time I have never been certain whether the moral of the Icarus story should only be, as is generally accepted, "don't try to fly too high," or whether it might also be thought of as "forget the wax and feathers, and do a better job on the wings."
—*Stanley Kubrick,* director

Some psychological studies suggest that more attractive people ascend corporate ranks faster and take more risks in life than unattractive people. Of course, attractiveness doesn't necessarily mean classical beauty. Your personality can make you attractive. It may mean that you have a warm smile, a confident posture, an inquisitive mind, a reputation for honesty and dependability. Should you also pay attention to how you look? Yes, if you believe the old standby that you can "dress for success" or "look the part."

PROJECTING
YOUR IMAGE

∽

*In order to be successful, one must
project an image of success at all times.*
—**Alan Ball**, *screenwriter, in*
American Beauty

∽

*Always have a great tan and wear a good
tuxedo with a glass of champagne . . .*
—**Robin Leach,**
television producer, host, and writer

∽

MAKE A GOOD FIRST IMPRESSION

Don't think that computers and cell phones have diminished the importance of physical presence.

Get a good handshake. You'll never forget the handshake of a person if it's bad. . . I shook hands within the last six months with a presidential candidate, who will remain nameless, whose handshake was frightening . . . Shine your shoes. First things I notice when somebody comes in is the handshake, and are their shoes shined?. . . . Be interesting, find things that make you an interesting person and don't be afraid to pass it on to people.

—**Brian Lamb**, founder and CEO of C-SPAN

"It's good to meet you" is only believable if your voice, tone, and warm, sincere smile match your words. This line doesn't play well through a frown, or even through a look of indifference.

Eye contact and being in the moment are critical in building support . . . A roving eye gives the impression of an insincere, hand-pumping Mr. Sleaze. People always remember the room surfer.

—**Susan RoAne**, writer and communications coach

Some emphasize the connection between physical attractiveness and success.

> From infancy to adulthood, beautiful people are treated preferentially and viewed more positively. This is true for men as well as women . . . Beauty conveys modest but real social advantages . . .
> —*Nancy Etcoff,* psychologist

When you wake up in the morning, you're relatively objective about what the day has in store for you— sometimes you're more apprehensive, sometimes you're more optimistic, sometimes you're less. But as you're getting dressed, if you look in the mirror and you think that you look great, then you're going to be as good as you can be. But if you think you look clumsy or awkward, you might as well just go out and get hit by a car, because you don't have a chance. In other words, how you see yourself is the way you'll end up being. Not taking those few moments in the morning to decide what you're saying to people by how you're choosing to dress is a lost opportunity.
—*Kenneth Cole,* clothing designer

BE SMART

You may look good and have a firm handshake, but are you up to the task? Success requires intelligence, another concept that challenges definition. Bill Gates has a take on what an intelligent presence is like:

It's an elusive concept. There's a certain sharpness, an ability to absorb new facts. To walk into a situation, have something explained to you and immediately say, "Well, what about this?" To ask an insightful question. To absorb it in real time. A capacity to remember. To relate to domains that may not seem connected at first. A certain creativity that allows people to be effective.

—*Bill Gates,* founder of Microsoft

Quality questions create a quality life. Successful people ask better questions, and as a result, they get better answers.

—*Anthony Robbins,* motivational speaker and management consultant

BE CONFIDENT

Thinking you are successful, or are destined to become successful, may have something do with convincing others that you're extraordinary.

History will be kind to me, for I intend to write it.
—*Winston Churchill,* former prime minister of Great Britain

෴

Early in life I had to choose between honest arrogance and hypocritical humility. I chose the former and have seen no reason to change.
—*Frank Lloyd Wright,* architect

෴

I have never known a man who died from overwork, but many who died from doubt.
—*Charles Horace Mayo,* surgeon and cofounder of the Mayo Clinic

෴

I think I absolutely knew I was gonna be famous. I knew from when I first wrote my first song about the first love of my life, and sat there on my bed and watched myself play it in the mirror with tears running down my face. It was on my 16th birthday—my mom and dad gave me my Goya classical guitar that day. I sat down, wrote this song, and I just knew that that was the only thing I could ever really do—write songs and sing them to people.

—**Stevie Nicks,** singer

Having a well-developed ego, contrary to popular opinion, is a positive attribute. It is the center of our consciousness and serves to give us a sense of purpose. I remember saying to someone, "Show me someone with no ego and I'll show you a big loser." I was trying to stir things up and provoke a reaction, but I later realized the basic idea is on target.

—**Donald Trump,** real estate magnate

Whatever I did, I wanted to be the best at it. I remember that moment in *The Natural* when Robert Redford says, "I just want to walk down the street and have people say, 'There goes Roy Hobbs, the best there ever was.'" So I was talking to my mother one day—this was when I was sixteen or seventeen—and she goes, "Matt, why are you so obsessed with acting?" And I said, "Because someday I want to walk down the street and have people say, 'There goes Matt Damon, the best there ever was.'"

—**Matt Damon,** actor, producer, and screenwriter

Jack Welch credits his mother for giving him his renowned self-esteem.

> Perhaps the greatest gift she [Grace Welch] gave me was self-confidence. It's what I looked for and tried to build in every executive who has ever worked with me. Confidence gives you courage and extends your reach. It lets you take greater risks and achieve far more than you ever thought possible.
>
> —*John (Jack) Welch, Jr.*, former chairman and CEO of General Electric

Welch had a stuttering problem as he was growing up that might have crippled his self-confidence if he didn't have so much of it:

> My mother served up the perfect excuse for my stuttering. "It's because you're so smart," she would tell me. "No one's tongue could keep up with a brain like yours." For years, in fact, I never worried about my stammer. I believed what she told me: that my mind worked faster than my mouth.
>
> —*John (Jack) Welch, Jr.*, former chairman and CEO of General Electric

I realize that I don't have limits. Limits are always influences that come from outside, from people who don't believe in themselves and their abilities. I firmly believe in myself. I know that I can do whatever I want and that I'll always reach my goals.

—**Madonna**, *singer and actor*

Without the confidence to ask for what you want, you won't get it.

> . . . As a person—you don't have to be a rock star—if you don't like the situation you're in, you don't have to settle for it. Say you order roasted chicken and they serve it fried. That's not cool. You have to get it roasted like you want, or you leave. That's just life. I don't think there's anything wrong with that. Satisfaction is crucial.
>
> —**Macy Gray**, *singer*

BE DIRECT

Know how to get your message across clearly and with confidence.

> If you equivocate, it's an indication that you're unsure of yourself and what you're doing. It's also what politicians do all the time, and I find it inappropriate, insulting, and condescending.
> —**Donald Trump**, real estate magnate

⌘

If you have an important point to make, don't try to be subtle or clever. Use a pile driver. Hit the point once. Then come back and hit it again. Then hit it a third time—a tremendous whack.
—**Winston Churchill**, *former prime minister of Great Britain*

⌘

DON'T EXPECT TO BE
LIKED BY EVERYONE

Of course, it seems preferable for everyone to like you and identify with you, but that's impossible. Anyhow, if that's your primary goal, you may find yourself being known as a pushover, a waffler, a sycophant.

If you spend your life deferring to someone else, you lose yourself in service. Is that what you want out of your life? It's a high price to pay just to be liked.
—*Judy Sheindlin (Judge Judy)*, judge and television celebrity

I don't know the key to success, but the key to failure is trying to please everybody.
—*William (Bill) Cosby, Jr.,* actor

. . . I say what I think, and I stand behind what I say. And I think it's a waste of time for people to be interviewed, and say things that they think other people want to hear. Or try and come off in a certain way. So I try to be as honest as I can be. And a lot of people make whatever judgments they're gonna make about that.
—*Gwyneth Paltrow,* actor

GET A REPUTATION
FOR BEING HONEST

One important lesson from the corporate scandals that have shamed the business world is that a reputation for honesty is crucial. This affects individuals as well as corporations and may mean forfeiting a short-term success in light of long-term repercussions.

Integrity is so perishable in the summer months of success.

—*Vanessa Redgrave*, actor

∽

Success without honor is an unseasoned dish; it will satisfy your hunger, but it won't taste good.

—*Joe Paterno*, football coach

∽

Don't cheat. That's why I got involved playing golf. There's something about that sport; people very seldom cheat in their game.

—*Scott McNealy*, chairman and
CEO of Sun Microsystems

∽

I think one lesson that we've all learned, and our company has certainly learned it in spades, is that reputational risk is every bit as important if not more important than credit risk and market risk. We understand that sometimes it's very important to look at what you do and say, "Jeez, while this may be legal, how would this look if it was on the front page of the paper three years from now?" Would you want to do that? And in some cases walk away from business today because that might affect your reputation, which is going to affect your ability to do business in a big way in the future.

—*Sanford (Sandy) Weill,* chairman of Citigroup

My father also taught me that reputation, not money, was the most important thing in the world. I heard this over and over in all kinds of situations. If I told a fib or did something wrong around the house or school, he'd reiterate it. He said, "you know, when you die, the only thing you're going to die with is the reputation you created as a person when you lived. All the money in the world isn't going to make you a better person. You're going to be respected and remembered for the type of person you were and the character you had. So, be truthful, be honest, and be a good neighbor."

—*William Rosenberg,* founder of Dunkin' Donuts

It is decidedly not true that "nice guys finish last," as that highly original American baseball philosopher, Leo Durocher, was once alleged to have said. . . .I do not deny that many appear to have succeeded in a material way by cutting corners and manipulating associates, both in their professional and in their personal lives. But material success is possible in this world and far more satisfying when it comes without exploiting others. The true measure of a career is to be able to be content, even proud, that you succeeded through your own endeavors without leaving a trail of casualties in your wake. . . .

—**Alan Greenspan,** *chairman of the*
U.S. Federal Reserve

Formula for success: Underpromise and overdeliver.
—*Tom Peters*, management consultant and writer

Success on any major scale requires you to accept responsibility . . . in the final analysis, the one quality that all successful people have . . . is the ability to take on responsibility.
—*Michael Korda*, publisher

Talk is cheap unless you can deliver.
—*Dana Elaine Owens (Queen Latifah)*, singer

Noneofushaveareal understanding of where we are heading. . . But decisions don't wait; investment decisions or personal decisions don't wait for that picture to be clarified. You have to make them when you have to make them. And try not to get too depressed in the journey, because there's a professional responsibility. If you are depressed, you can't motivate your staff to extraordinary measures. So you have to keep your own spirits up even though you well understand that you don't know what you're doing.
—*Andrew (Andy) Grove*, chairman of Intel

If you want to be thought of as a solid, reliable pillar of your community when you're 50, you can't be an irresponsible, corner-cutting exploiter at 25. . . . The time to worry about your reputation is before you have one. You determine your reputation by deciding who and what you are and by keeping that lofty vision of yourself in mind, even when you're having a rip-roaring good time.

—**William Raspberry**, *writer and Pulitzer Prize winner*

HAVE AT LEAST ONE HUGE
ACCOMPLISHMENT TO YOUR NAME

It only takes one huge success to get a good reputation. Your future success will grow on that one big feat. Here, economist Merton Miller gives an example of this phenomenon.

I always use an example that dates back to the '30s. The big name then was Bernard Baruch. A genius. He was everybody's favorite pundit. There wasn't any economic issue where the press didn't go to see Barney. When you study his fabulous record, however, I think he was right once. But, he was right in a big way. If you make a big score way out on the right-hand tail of the distribution, then the probabilities you face from then on are mostly the little moves to the left and to the right in the center of the distribution. You're not going to get that first big gain removed. You only need to make one big score in finance to be a hero forever.

—*Merton Miller,* economist and
Nobel Prize winner in Economics

GUARD YOUR IMAGE

Once you become known for something and you develop your own personal formula for success, it may be difficult to change the ingredients. Comedian Andrew Dice Clay abandoned his controversial image when he agreed to host a network show under the condition that he tone down his act.

> You know how everybody's got to pay their bills, well I had to pay my bills. So, I took a network show where they told me drop the Dice attitude and the Dice name so the sponsors get behind it, and I told them, "If you do that then you're making a big mistake, 'cause the show ain't gonna last." . . . And it didn't.
> —*Andrew Dice Clay*, comedian

Some successful people like to preserve their image by withdrawing from public life. When asked to explain his aversion to publicity, writer Don DeLillo said:

> I just want to keep a little bit of anonymity. Television consumes the things it shows. It replaces reality.
> —*Don DeLillo*, writer

BE FUNNY

Have a sense of humor. All successful people tend to have a sense of the absurd about themselves. They laugh easily, and recognize that we all have foibles which can at times be very humorous. In other words, don't take yourself too seriously.

—*Joe DiBaggio,* president of Tufts University

I always tell my wife, Shelby, that if she's going to be cruel to me, do it in the form of a joke. That helps the sting. But it still has to be funny.

—*Tom Arnold,* writer, producer, and actor

Keep your sense of humor. There's enough stress in the rest of your life to let bad shots ruin a game you're supposed to enjoy.

—*Amy Strum Alcott,* golfer

You can look at success as a balance of forces and counterforces: passion vs. discipline; flashes of inspiration vs. months or years of plodding hard work. You won't succeed if one dramatically outweighs the other. Just when things start going well and your ego starts to swell, there's another force you'll reckon with: feedback. Feedback comes in many forms, including criticism, advice, and hard numbers. Feedback will ground you, keep your ego in check, and help you refine your goals and make improvements.

GETTING FEEDBACK

cxo

*I have always found that being an
attentive listener can be valuable in life.
When I was younger, a number
of people, including my older brothers,
gave me helpful pieces of advice. As I have
entered a life of public service,
my constituents have provided me with their
positions on a number of issues.
Their opinions are essential. . .*
—**Edward Kennedy,** *U.S. senator*

cxo

*As every cockroach knows, thriving
on poisons is the secret of success.*
—**Mason Cooley,** *aphorist*

TAME YOUR EGO

Don't let your ego get in the way of genuine constructive criticism. Feedback can come from colleagues, customers, employees, friends—anyone who experiences some aspect of your work.

> It takes humility to seek feedback. It takes wisdom to understand it, analyze it, and appropriately act on it.
> —*Stephen R. Covey,* management consultant and motivational speaker

> . . . I think that one of the greatest sins of character almost everybody is vulnerable to is pride. And we all tend to look at other people who do things we don't agree with or think are bad things and say, well, whatever is wrong with me, at least I'm not that. And I think sometimes we are too harsh on other people because it's like a crutch, we don't have to deal with whatever is going on in our lives. And I think it has really helped me to be less judgmental and less hypocritical.
> —*William (Bill) Clinton,* U.S. president

Listen to feedback with an open mind. If you become indignant or defensive, you won't benefit.

> I seldom get self-righteous, and even when I am being impolite (almost always on purpose—there's

an art to insulting people, too), I tend to try to not be too serious about it. And most of the time it means that I can take criticism constructively, and sometimes just change my opinion on the fly and laugh at myself over having turned on a dime.

—*Linus Torvalds,* founder of Linux

And this was what the most respected and widely read television critic, Tom Shales, wrote in the *Washington Post.* "O'Brien is a living collage of annoying nervous habits. He giggles and jiggles about and fiddles with his cuffs . . . Let the *Late Show with Conan O'Brien* become the late Late Show, and may the host return to whence he came." There's more, but it gets kind of mean.

Needless to say, I took a lot of criticism, some of it deserved, some of it excessive, and, to be honest with you, it hurt like you would not believe. But I'm telling you all this for a reason. I've had a lot of success. I've had a lot of failure. I've looked good. I've looked bad. I've been praised. And I've been criticized. But my mistakes have been necessary.

—*Conan O'Brien,* television host,
comedian, and producer

ACT ON YOUR FEEDBACK

Determine if the feedback will help you. If so, implement it.

> We really rely on our users for their feedback, which enables us to determine what new services to offer and what cities to expand to. We don't expand to new cities with any scientific process. We review requests for new cities in our feedback forum and other mechanisms. If we figure that a particular city has a high broadband penetration, and if it looks like it will help people in those cities, then we will put it up.
> —*Craig Newmark,* founder of Craigslist.org

Practice damage control. If you actively seek criticism, you can defend yourself and your work better than if criticism takes you by surprise. This is how Charles Darwin preempted opposition to his ideas.

> I had . . . during many years followed a golden rule, namely, that whenever a published fact, a new observation or thought came across me, which was opposed to my general results, to make a memorandum of it without fail and at once; for I had found by experience that such facts and thoughts were far more apt to escape from the memory than favourable ones. Owing to this habit, very few objections were raised against my views which I had not at least noticed and attempted to answer.
> —*Charles Darwin,* naturalist

KEEP IT ALL IN CHECK

Don't let criticism eliminate your drive. At the same time, don't let your fear of criticism prevent you from seeking feedback.

> Others have the opposite problem . . . egos that too readily let themselves be quashed by all the fire-snorting fellows stomping around. These people tend (understandably) to keep their creativity more private. That makes it hard for them to seek critical feedback, the grist for self-improvement. At either extreme, ego can be more curse than blessing.
>
> —*David Brin,* writer

Perhaps more dangerous than criticism is excessive praise. From it you'll learn nothing. Saul Bellow said the following in his acceptance speech for the Nobel Prize in Literature:

> For when I am praised on all sides I worry a bit. I remember the scriptural warning, "Woe unto you when all men shall speak well of you." Universal agreement seems to open the door to dismissal. We know how often our contemporaries are mistaken. They are not invariably wrong, but it is not at all a bad idea to remember that they can't confer immortality on you. Immortality—a chilling thought. I feel that I have scarcely begun to master my trade.
>
> But I need not worry too much that all men will speak well of me. The civilized community agrees

that there is no higher distinction than the Nobel Prize but it agrees on little else, so I need not fear that the doom of universal approval is hanging over me. When I publish a book I am often roundly walloped by reviewers—a disagreeable but necessary corrective to self-inflation.

—*Saul Bellow,* Nobel Prize winner in Literature

Being fearless means em-bracing risks, forging ahead on an uncertain path, and being courageous. Fearlessness requires self-confidence. It forces you to do things others wouldn't do if confronted with the same circumstances. Fearlessness is shocking nerve, steel stomach, indestructible backbone. It's galling chutzpah, unblinking vision, and Teflon-like resilience.

So, how do you get that way?

BEING FEARLESS

Success is the child of audacity.
—**Benjamin Disraeli**, *former Prime minister of Great Britain*

❧

Living fearlessly is not the same thing as never being afraid. It's good to be afraid occasionally. Fear is a great teacher. What's not good is living in fear, allowing fear to dictate your choices, allowing fear to define who you are. Living fearlessly means standing up to fear, taking its measure, refusing to let it shape and define your life. Living fearlessly means taking risks, taking gambles, not playing it safe. It means refusing to take "no" for an answer when you are sure that the answer should have been "yes." It means refusing to settle for less than what is your due, what is yours by right, what is yours by the sweat of your labor and your effort.
—**Michael Ignatieff**, *writer and historian*

❧

Life shrinks or expands in proportion to one's courage.
—**Anaïs Nin**, *writer*

❧

Once you let go of the idea that there's only one right way to do things, you'll be less fearful of doing the wrong thing.

As I think back over the years, I have been guided by four principles for decision making. First, that there is no certainty. Second, every decision, as a consequence, is a matter of weighing probabilities. Third, despite uncertainty we must decide and we must act. And lastly, we must evaluate decisions not just on the results, but how they are made.

—*Robert Rubin,* former U.S. Secretary of the Treasury

. . . I also recognize that part of my job as a Christian is to recognize that I may not always be right, that God doesn't speak to me alone, . . . And I guess I think to myself, you know, I have to struggle a little bit more and admit that certain human fallibility, and not assert my unyielding confidence that I always know the truth.

—*Barack Obama,* U.S. senator

OVERCOME THE FEAR OF FAILURE

Imagine how you would live your life if you stopped fearing failure.

To be ambitious for wealth, and yet always expecting to be poor; to be always doubting your ability to get what you long for, is like trying to reach east by traveling west. There is no philosophy which will help man to succeed when he is always doubting his ability to do so, and thus attracting failure. No matter how hard you work for success, if your thought is saturated with the fear of failure, it will kill your effort, neutralize your endeavors, and make success impossible.

—*Charles Baudouin,* psychiatrist and writer

We gain strength, and courage, and confidence by each experience in which we really stop to look fear in the face . . . we must do that which we think we cannot.

—*Eleanor Roosevelt,* diplomat and First Lady

Teddy Roosevelt suggests that the payoff is always worth the price, because it's more honorable to try and fail than not to try and fail.

∽

It is not the critic who counts, not the man who points out how the strong man stumbled, or where the doer of deeds could have done better. The credit belongs to the man who is actually in the arena; whose face is marred by the dust and sweat and blood; who strives valiantly; who errs and comes short again and again; who knows the great enthusiasms, the great devotions, and spends himself in a worthy course; who at the best, knows in the end the triumph of high achievement, and who, at worst, if he fails, at least fails while daring greatly; so that his place shall never be with those cold and timid souls who know neither victory nor defeat.

—**Theodore Roosevelt**, *U.S. president*

∽

HAVE A LIFE-CHANGING EXPERIENCE—
OR ACT AS IF YOU HAD ONE

It's not uncommon for people who have undergone life-changing experiences such as a disease, a stressful situation, or the loss of a loved one to see life differently. Sometimes, the experience drives them to be more fearless than they would be otherwise. They regard life as limited and make the most of it. If this hasn't happened to you, try to live as if it did.

☙

Cancer taught me a plan for more purposeful living, and that in turn taught me how to train and to win more purposefully. It taught me that pain has a reason, and that sometimes the experience of losing things—whether health or a car or an old sense of self—has its own value in the scheme of life. Pain and loss are great enhancers.

—*Lance Armstrong*, bicyclist

☙

I had the confidence, because when I was very small my mother threw me in the ocean and watched without moving as I struggled to survive. She watched as I screamed, yelled, gulped, and flailed in a panic-stricken effort to stay afloat. She watched as I clawed desperately at the water, unable to manage for more than a few seconds before starting to sink below the surface. She watched as the ocean swallowed me, second by second. Then, mercifully, my father's hands reached under, fished me out, and handed me back to my mother . . . who threw me back in again and again, until she was convinced that I knew how to swim."

—**Sidney Poitier**, *actor*

ↀ

BE EXPERIMENTAL

It's OK to improvise.

> . . . I guess I'm not easily inhibited by the fact that I don't know something about a subject. It doesn't stop me from dabbling in it; everybody has to learn it for the first time, so why not?
>
> —*Joshua Lederberg*, Nobel Prize winner in Medicine

Lack of experience didn't stop Katharine Hepburn at a crucial casting. She improvised and her experiment paid off.

They had sent for me to be the understudy to the leading lady. Naturally, I was thrilled. I learned the part and sat on the sidelines quite convinced that I would be far superior to the leading lady I was watching, Lucile Nikolas. She was a very competent actress who did not have the advantage of being very young and absolutely outrageous and full of a sort of wild confidence based on nothing but energy and ego. Of course I thought I was scared to death, but all I can say now, looking back, is that I was not scared enough. Open a door, I'd go through. Even if the room I was entering was on fire. One lunch hour, after the play had been in rehearsal for a week, they asked me to stay and play a scene. Pushed by some frenetic boiling-over, I must have read it very well. They fired the leading lady and took me. I didn't of course know what I was doing but I did it with great style.

—**Katharine Hepburn,** actor

Be comfortable with the idea of looking foolish. You're just experimenting.

. . . . So whatever you want to do, just do it. Don't worry about making a damn fool of yourself. Making a damn fool of yourself is absolutely essential. And you will have a great time.

—**Gloria Steinem,** writer and feminist

Some see fearless experimentation as a requirement of growing up.

So you shouldn't waste your creative twenties trying to get over personal hang-ups that you should have resolved in your adolescent years. These are your most creative years. You'll have more judgment, more wisdom later on. But your creative bursts—the kind of directions that you are going to follow in life; the kind of innovations, the ideas, the willingness to ask the impertinent questions: That's what your twenties will afford you.

—**Ralph Nader,** consumer advocate, activist, and politician

GAIN CONFIDENCE FROM
PAST SUCCESSES

Once you have a few achievements to your name, draw strength from them to accomplish future goals.

> Self-esteem must be earned! When you dare to dream, dare to follow that dream, dare to suffer through the pain, sacrifice, self-doubts, and friction from the world, you will genuinely impress yourself.
>
> —*Laura Schlessinger,* radio talk show host

Entrepreneur Richard Branson's mother would assign grueling tasks to her children. Branson credits his successful completion of these tasks as giving him the confidence to take on seemingly insurmountable tasks later in his life. Among his accomplishments are founding a business empire that includes Virgin Records and Virgin Atlantic Airways, manning the first hot air balloon ever to cross the Atlantic Ocean, and hosting his own reality TV show.

> My mother was determined to make us independent. When I was four, she stopped the car a few miles from our house and made me find my own way home across the fields. My youngest sister Vanessa's earliest memory is being woken up in the dark one January morning because Mum had decided that I should cycle to Bournemouth that day. Bournemouth

was fifty miles away from home in Shamley Green, Surrey. I was under twelve, but Mum thought that it would teach me the importance of stamina and a sense of direction. I remember setting off in the dark and I have a vague recollection of staying with night with a relative. I have no idea how I found their house or how I got back to Shamley Green, but I do remember finally walking back into the kitchen like a conquering hero, feeling tremendously proud of my marathon bike ride and expecting a huge welcome.

"Well done, Ricky," Mum greeted me in the kitchen, where she was chopping onions. "Was that fun? Now, could you run along to the vicar's? He's got some logs he wants chopping, and I told him that you'd be back any minute."
—*Richard Branson,* entrepreneur and founder of the Virgin brand

STAND UP FOR YOURSELF

Inevitably, someone will say something or do something to inhibit your success. You can cower in fear. Or you can stand up for yourself. Hillary Rodham Clinton relays this lesson her mother taught her.

"Go back out there," she ordered, "and if Suzy hits you, you have my permission to hit her back. You have to stand up for yourself. There's no room in this house for cowards." She later told me she watched from behind the dining room curtain as I squared my shoulders and marched across the street.

I returned a few minutes later, glowing with victory. "I can play with the boys now." I said. "And Suzy will be my friend."

She was and she still is.
—*Hillary Rodham Clinton*, U.S. senator

Few have understood fearless defiance as well as writer Salman Rushdie, who had a fatwa (death sentence) placed on him by Ayatollah Khomeini, the leader of Iran, who deemed Rushdie's book, *The Satanic Verses*, "blasphemous against Islam." Here, Rushdie implores you to "thumb your noses" against the forces that inspire fear.

∽

. . . *In the years to come you will find yourselves up against gods of all sorts, big and little gods, corporate and incorporeal gods, all of them demanding to be worshipped and obeyed—the myriad deities of money and power, of convention and custom, that will seek to limit and control your thoughts and lives. Defy them; that's my advice to you. Thumb your noses; cock your snooks. For, as the myths tell us, it is by defying the gods that human beings have best expressed their humanity.*

—**Salman Rushdie**, writer

∽

Midway in your pursuit of success, something may happen (or fail to happen) and you may think that you had been deluding yourself about a happy ending. Every successful person has experienced failure. It's just part of taking risks. If—and when—you fail to reach a goal or disappoint yourself and others, remember the words of Michael Jordan, John Lennon, Katharine Graham, John Travolta, and other occasional failures.

SURVIVING
SETBACKS

SUCCESS is counted sweetest
By those who ne'er succeed.
To comprehend a nectar
Requires sorest need.
Not one of all the purple host
Who took the flag to-day
Can tell the definition,
So clear, of victory,
As he, defeated, dying,
On whose forbidden ear
The distant strains of triumph
Break, agonized and clear.
—**Emily Dickinson**, *poet*

EMBRACE FAILURE

Many successful people seem to count occasional failure as a requirement of success.

Success is how high you bounce when you've hit bottom.
—*General George S. Patton Jr.,* general

Success is the ability to go from failure to failure without losing your enthusiasm.
—*Winston Churchill,* former prime minister of Great Britain

Only those who dare to fail greatly, can ever achieve greatly.
—*Robert F. (Bobby) Kennedy,* U.S. attorney general

We are born naked and helpless and are driven to learn by trial and error. We make mistakes, but that is healthy if you have the courage to admit you've made a mistake.
—*R. Buckminster Fuller,* architect and inventor

Of the many celebrities who believe failure is essential for success is writer and radio host Garrison Keillor.

> We need to talk about the pursuit of failure, I think. A person who does not know failure is a person with a poor sense of reality. A person who goes through his twenties and thirties racking up one prize after another, getting the great job and the beautiful size 4 wife and the starter mansion and the two beautiful, gifted children with the Celtic names, is a man who is headed for a gigantic midlife crisis in which he runs away with a waitress named Misty and perms his hair and becomes a 45-year-old singer/songwriter. You don't want that.
>
> —*Garrison Keillor,* writer and radio host

Basketball player Michael Jordan carries the same message:

> I have missed more than 9,000 shots in my career. I have lost almost 300 games. On 26 occasions I have been entrusted to take the game-winning shot . . . and I missed. I have failed over and over and over again in my life. And that's precisely why I succeed.
>
> —*Michael Jordan,* basketball player

Actor John Malkovich sees failure as the only certainty in his profession.

> It's not a field, I think, for people who need to have success every day; if you can't live with a nightly sort of disaster, you should get out. I wouldn't describe myself as lacking in confidence, but I would just say that . . . the ghosts you chase you never catch.
> —*John Malkovich*, actor

∾

Would you like me to give you a formula for success? It's quite simple, really. Double your rate of failure. You're thinking of failure as the enemy of success. But it isn't at all. You can be discouraged by failure—or you can learn from it. So go ahead and make mistakes. Make all you can. Because, remember that's where you'll find success.
—**Thomas J. Watson**, *founder of IBM*

∾

ACT ON YOUR SETBACKS

How to turn failure to success? Have the right attitude about it.

It's not what happens to you, it's how you react to it.
—***William (Bill) Clinton***, U.S. president

Forget your personal tragedy. We are all bitched from the start and you especially have to be hurt like hell before you can write seriously. But when you get the damned hurt, use it—don't cheat with it. Be as faithful to it as a scientist—but don't think anything is of any importance because it happens to you or anyone belonging to you.
—***Ernest Hemingway***, writer

Develop success from failures. Discouragement and failure are two of the surest stepping stones to success.
—***Dale Carnegie***, lecturer and author

When the Beatles were depressed, we had this thing that I would chant and they would answer. It was from a cheap movie they made about Liverpool years ago. And in it they would say, "Where are we going, Johnny," or something and the leader of the gang would say, "we're going to burn this" or "we're going to stomp on that." Well, I would say to the others when we were all depressed thinking that the group was going nowhere, this is a shitty deal, we're in a shitty dressing room—I would say, "where are we going, fellows?" And they would say, "To the toppermost of the poppermost." I would say, "Right!" And we would all cheer up.

—**John Lennon**, *singer and musician*

SEE THE WHOLE

Surviving setbacks means stepping back to see the whole of a situation. Be reflective. This gives you perspective, which in turn gives you control.

I made mistakes and suffered great distress from them, partly because I believed that if you just worked diligently enough you wouldn't make mistakes. I truly believed that other people in my position didn't make mistakes; I couldn't see that everybody makes them, even people with great experience. What I did that I'm certain my male counterparts did not, and which is particularly tormenting, was to lie awake at night reliving the events of the day, going over and over certain scenes, wondering how I could have managed whatever it was differently.

—*Katharine Graham,* president of
The Washington Post

Exercise your ability to tune out the chatter.

. . . If you come around me and tell me bad news all the time, I can say, "You know what? I don't want to hear it." If it's just gossip, you know, I can choose not to hear it. And that, in effect, can control my mood.

—*John Travolta,* actor

. . . Every once in a while, like when a tabloid claims I'm a heroin addict and he knows I'm anti-drugs, my brother'll call and go, "What's going on?" It's kind of like getting caught in an amazing machine. But you have to laugh . . . What I've gone through has only made me stronger. Anything you survive does. And I've learned a lot of lessons about patience and separating myself from all the garbage. One of them is that you have to believe that everything is a blessing, even if it's one in disguise. You can get through it if you trust that it's all for a reason.

—*Pamela Anderson,* actor

Filmmaker Deepa Mehta suffered a terrible setback when a mob ransacked the set of her film *Water,* the controversial story of an Indian widow falling in love with a lower-caste man. Then she found a source of inspiration that helped her gain perspective and move on.

I felt I never wanted to make another film again. It was so painful, so terrible and dark, and so utterly unnecessary. I was questioning my craft. Suddenly I was no longer just a filmmaker but a controversial filmmaker, which is very scary. Then I heard a story about an East Indian businessman who had gone to the casino at Niagara and was playing the slots. He sat next to a woman. They started talking, and he said, "Who are you?" And she said she was East Indian. An Indian woman alone and in such a place, he didn't believe her. He said, "You can't be," and she said, "I can be whoever you want me to be." That story was like a bolt of lightning.

—*Deepa Mehta,* director, producer, and screenwriter

Seeing the whole often gives you insight to turn failure on its head. Whenever an experiment failed for scientist Jonas Salk, he said he made a discovery.

As I look upon the experience of an experimentalist, everything that you do is, in a sense, succeeding. It's telling you what not to do, as well as what to do. Not infrequently, I go into the laboratory, and people would say something didn't work. And I say, "Great, we've made a great discovery!" If you thought it was going to work, and it didn't work, that tells you as much as if it did. So my attitude is not one of pitfalls; my attitude is one of challenges and "What is nature telling me?"

—*Jonas Salk,* physician, research scientist,
 and developer of the polio vaccine

Poker king Phil Hellmuth regards setbacks as part of the gamble for success:

> I think that that's the cycle of life that anyone who steps into a great amount of success at an early age is going to experience, and they go one of two ways. I think most people, when they experience their downsides—because it's not all about being straight up—become much more deep and interesting and reflective. I hate the lows in poker, but I love the way that they helped me become a better man.
>
> —*Phil Hellmuth,* winner of the World Series in Poker

Survive a setback by getting a different perspective—literally. Making a physical move, as comedian Ellen DeGeneres did at one low point in her career, may translate into making a mental move. Exercise is also important (see the next chapter on managing stress and anxiety).

> I was hurt and thought, I'd rather live on a farm. So I went to Ojai. It was a really important thing to do for myself, growthwise—I think I came back with a little bit of maturity. I've worked for 20 years to get where I am.
>
> —*Ellen DeGeneres,* comedian

Physicist Brian Greene believes the same about his life work in an area of physics known as string theory, which has yet to be proven correct—and has suffered setbacks. To him, the knowledge discovered in the process makes it all worthwhile.

I and many others, however, would not feel it had been a waste of time if the theory turns out to be wrong, because we've developed a lot of important mathematics. We've developed connections to other, more well-established areas of physics, which I think will be important in their own right. We will have done some very valuable work. To me, if the theory turns out to be right, that will be tremendously thick and tasty icing on the cake, but without that icing, to me the work will still have been incredibly interesting and useful.

—*Brian Greene*, physicist

REALIZE THAT TIME
CHANGES PERCEPTIONS

Filmmaker Stanley Kubrick and writer Jhumpa Lahiri remind us that initial failures can turn into wild success.

The first reviews of *2001* were insulting, let alone bad. An important Los Angeles critic faulted *Paths of Glory* because the actors didn't speak with French accents. When *Dr. Strangelove* came out, a New York paper ran a review under the head MOSCOW COULD NOT BUY MORE HARM TO AMERICA. Something like that. But critical opinion on my films has always been salvaged by what I would call subsequent critical opinion.
—*Stanley Kubrick*, director and producer

I started writing, and then I bought a book on where to send stories. I would send them out, they all came back, then I would write something else, this went on for years. Sometimes I got a nice note, and that gives you a little bit of inspiration for the next time you sit down to write. It's a combination of being attuned to that whole world out there, the editor, the publisher, blah, blah, blah, but also knowing that really is not the goal. If it happens, it happens; if it doesn't happen for a long time, that's okay too.
—*Jhumpa Lahiri*, writer

Stress isn't always bad. For many, it's a necessary part of the process. Stress can be a motivator. The pressure of deadlines, budgets, and the demands of others can push one to accomplish something that would have been impossible with unlimited time, money, and the absence of pressure. Stress can be good. The important part is keeping it in check.

MANAGING STRESS

*The process of living is
the process of reacting to stress.*
—**Stanley Sarnoff**, *physiologist*

*Pray that success will not come any
faster than you are able to endure it.*
—**Elbert Hubbard**, *writer*

STOP SEEKING PERFECTION

The most successful people know that they can't control everything. The fear of uncertainty is one of the biggest causes of stress.

How do you know what is the right path to choose to get the result that you desire? And the honest answer is this. You won't. And accepting that greatly eases the anxiety of your life experience.

—*Jonathan (Jon) Stewart,* actor, writer, comedian, and television host

Computer programmer James Gosling notes that you might never find perfection. Simply do the best you can.

If you go to the Santa Cruz Beach Boardwalk, there is this game called Whack-a-Mole. It's a table with 16 holes, and this little mechanical mole sticks his head out of one of the holes for a second. You whack it with a bat. He pops his head up, and you whack him, and he pops up someplace else. . . . Engineering design is like playing Whack-a-Mole. You have a problem sticking up over there. You go and whack it, and it goes away. But have you really fixed it, or has it just moved somewhere else? It's often hard to tell whether you've solved the problem or moved the problem . . . . It's almost a truism that you never actually find a perfect answer to a problem. You just find the answer that has the least problems.

—*James Gosling,* computer programmer and inventor of Java

DEAL WITH THE CAUSE OF THE STRESS

If you're getting too stressed, immediately deal with the cause of your distress. Don't always avoid it by going golfing or turning on the TV. If you do, you're just displacing the stress. In the end, you'll only be hit harder.

If I find that some particular thing is causing me to have stress, that's a warning flag for me. What it means is there's something that I haven't completely identified, perhaps in my conscious mind that is bothering me, and I haven't yet taken any action on it. I find as soon as I identify it, and make the first phone call, or send off the first e-mail message, or whatever it is that we're going to do to start to address that situation—even if it's not solved— the mere fact that we're addressing it dramatically reduces any stress that might come from it. So stress comes from ignoring things that you shouldn't be ignoring, I think, in large part.

—*Jeffrey Bezos,* founder and CEO of *Amazon.com*

BE PHILOSOPHICAL

Philosophizing about your stressful situation might help you transcend it.

When you find yourself stressed, ask yourself
one question:
Will this matter in 5 years from now?
If yes, then do something about the situation.
If no, then let it go.
—*Catherine Pulsifer*, writer

One of the symptoms of an approaching nervous breakdown is the belief that one's work is terribly important.
—*Bertrand Russell,* philosopher and
Nobel Prize winner in Literature

Rule Number 1 is, don't sweat the small stuff. Rule Number 2 is, it's all small stuff. And if you can't fight and you can't flee, flow.
—*Robert Eliot,* cardiologist

*Do not anticipate
trouble or worry about what
may never happen.
Keep in the sunlight.*

—**Benjamin Franklin**, statesman and inventor

KEEP A JOURNAL

Every successful person has his or her own ways of surviving stress. For many, keeping a journal helps in more than one way. It helps you articulate your feelings in the moment; the act of writing can be relaxing. And it will help you in the future when you want to look back and gain perspective on your actions.

I discovered as a very young man that my way of writing was to talk to myself, as it were. In everything I've written since I began to write professionally, I adopted a habit of putting down my thoughts and arguments, my impressions, my experiences, to myself in diary form, in journal form. Somehow the bits of writing to myself made it easier for me to uncover things which in a more formal writing I might have overlooked . . . And then I found, as keepers of journals often do, it was solace in times of great trouble. It was a way of exploring, of looking at things I had not thought about before, precisely because a journal was so informal. I was not worried about what the public would think. So, it became simply my way of writing. I never bored myself. I found it always exciting. I still do.

—*Alfred Kazin,* writer and historian

KNOW WHAT CALMS YOU

Anticipate stress and know how to calm yourself when it happens. This will help you in many situations.

> Nobody gets through life without difficult things happening. We all have to know how to handle crisis. My father used to say to me, "Whenever you get into a jam, whenever you get into a crisis or an emergency, and everybody around you is getting very excited," he said, "You become the calmest person in the room and you'll be able to figure your way out of it. Force yourself to be calmer than you feel."
>
> —*Rudolph Giuliani,* politician and former mayor of New York City

How can you transcend your anxiety? For actor Harrison Ford, relaxation is flying a plane.

> Part of it certainly has to do with how different it is from the other things I do. And I think the focus and the concentration and the attention to detail that flying takes is a kind of meditation. I find it restful and engaging, and other things slip away.
>
> —*Harrison Ford,* actor

For singer Mick Jagger, it's moments of quiet reflection.

. . . In this busy life if you don't have these moments of repose, you can't have any enlightenment, small or large. It's very rare you're gonna have enlightenment when you're running around like a dervish, unless you're whirling in a cathedral. You need moments of repose to open yourself up to any kind of enlightenment. If you just wake up, grab your breakfast and run the rest of the day, and dance yourself silly until you collapse, you're probably not giving yourself any moment to let anything else in.

—*Mick Jagger,* singer

℗

Wherever you are, right now make no formal effort of any kind. Simply bring your awareness to the place where you are sitting. Be aware of yourself from head to toe. If your eyes close, let them close by themselves, lightly and simply relax your forehead.

Just relax your forehead, be still and bring your awareness to your breathing. Only bring the awareness to your breathing. Do nothing with your breath, only follow how the breath is flowing.

—*Swami Veda Bharati Maharaj,* yogi

Is success like a mountain;

once you peak you can only go downhill? Or is suc-

cess an endless upward projectile, a plodding uphill

battle? You may hope that your success is a series

of peaks. Perhaps you could tolerate plateaus. But

if you're like most people, you'll do anything to

avoid the plummets.

Every successful person has something to say

about maintaining his or her status. Not every suc-

cessful person has an answer.

STAYING
SUCCESSFUL

❧

The road to success is
always under construction.
—**Lily Tomlin**, *actor*

❧

Success is an absurd, erratic thing.
She arrives when one least expects her
and after she has come may depart again
almost because of a whim.
—**Alice Foote MacDougall**, *entrepreneur*

❧

I dread success. To have succeeded is
to have finished one's business on earth, like
the male spider, who is killed by the female
the moment he has succeeded in his
courtship. I like a state of continual becom-
ing, with a goal in front and not behind.
—**George Bernard Shaw**, *playwright*

❧

MEASURE YOUR SUCCESS

How do you determine if you've been successful in the first place? Find a standard that is meaningful to you.

Success is when reality exceeds expectations.
—*John D. Gerhart*, philanthropist and educator

Success is when you reach cruising altitude and the seat belt lights come off.
—*John Mayer*, musician

The measure of success is not whether you have a tough problem to deal with, but whether it is the same problem you had last year.
—*John Foster Dulles*, former U.S. secretary of state

Success to me is having ten honeydew melons, and eating only the top half of each one.
—*Barbra Streisand*, singer and actor

The logic of worldly success rests on a fallacy: the strange error that our perfection depends on the thoughts and opinions and applause of other men! A weird life it is, indeed, to be living always in somebody else's imagination, as if that were the only place in which one could at last become real!

—*Thomas Merton*, writer and poet

For some, success is measured by wealth.

. . . You have to measure success in terms of the bottom line, are you making a profit, are you balancing the books and breaking even first of all and then starting to make a profit. That's a measure of success really.

—*Marilyn Orcharton*, entrepreneur

For others, it's the impact they have on others.

I must admit that I personally measure success in terms of the contributions an individual makes to her or his fellow human beings.

—*Margaret Mead*, anthropologist

My grandfather told me when I was about ten, as we stood at the edge of a lake in Moodus, Connecticut, that each time I threw a stone into the water I was raising the level of the lake.

I threw another stone. It wasn't happening. So I threw a rock. I still couldn't see the level of the lake rising, but my grandfather asked me if I saw the ripple.

Years later I understood what he was getting at. The ripple is what we all have to be satisfied with. That's what we all have to work our hearts out for—to make a ripple. Then, we won't see it, but the water level does rise.
—**Norman Lear**, *television writer and producer*

For others, it's a change of attitude.

> You have reached the pinnacle of success as soon as you become uninterested in money, compliments, or publicity.
> —*Thomas Wolfe,* writer

> Success can make you go one of two ways. It can make you a prima donna—or it can smooth the edges, take away the insecurities, let the nice things come out.
> —*Barbara Walters,* talk show host

Howard Stevenson, a professor at Harvard Business School, and business ethicist Laura Nash offer these measures of success:

ACHIEVEMENT: Do you measure accomplishments against an external goal? Power, wealth, recognition, competition against others.

HAPPINESS: Is there contentment or pleasure with and about your life?

SIGNIFICANCE: Do you have a valued impact on others whom you choose?

LEGACY: Have you infused your values and your accomplishments into the lives of others to leave something behind?

> —*Howard Stevenson,* entrepreneur
> and professor, and *Laura Nash,* business ethicist

KEEP DEVELOPING YOUR SKILLS

The most crucial advice successful people have to offer the newly-initiated concerns the importance of working hard after a first success. You need to keep growing and acquiring new skills and dreaming up new ideas. It's human nature to rest on one's laurels. Heed the following warnings:

There is no point at which you can say, "Well, I'm successful now. I might as well take a nap."
—*Carrie Fisher,* actor

The toughest thing about success is that you've got to keep on being a success. Talent is only a starting point in this business. You've got to keep on working that talent. Someday I'll reach for it and it won't be there.
—*Irving Berlin,* composer and musician

Permanent success cannot be achieved except by incessant intellectual labour, always inspired by the ideal.
—*Sarah Bernhardt,* actor

If the rate of change on the outside exceeds the rate of change on the inside, the end is near.
—*John (Jack) Welch Jr.,* former chairman and CEO of General Electric

In 1967, Muriel Siebert became the first woman to purchase a seat on the New York Stock Exchange (NYSE). In 1969, she became the first woman to own and operate a brokerage firm that belonged to the NYSE. In 1977, she was named New York State banking superintendent. She continues to run her company, and practices the advice she dispenses here:

Technology will continue to march ahead, with or without you. I've been on Wall Street for over 40 years. If someone had told me even five years ago that I'd have a computer on my desk and actually use it every day, I would have laughed. Technology is changing everything, and that will not stop. Make technology your friend. Use it. Otherwise it will be your enemy.

But I also recommend that you keep your other skills sharp and current. Learn finance. Watch closely global economics. And know how to write and talk and read and listen.

—*Muriel Siebert,* founder and president of
Muriel Siebert & Co.

USE YOUR MOMENTUM

Once a success, always a success—with a little luck, effort, determination, support, good habits, hard work, and character.

Success breeds success. People want to be involved with things that are successful, that are moving forward. One of the ways the campaign has been able to maintain its momentum is because we always have strategies, plans of action, concrete things that both individuals and national campaigns can do. I believe that human beings tend—you know the lemming factor, move forward because everybody moves forward? If you tell the campaigns what the next steps they should consider for their national work are, then they tend to do them. And, that's been part of the success of the campaign.
—*Jody Williams,* activist and
Nobel Peace Prize winner

All paths lead to the same goal: to convey to others what we are. And we must pass through solitude and difficulty, isolation and silence in order to reach forth to the enchanted place where we can dance our clumsy dance and sing our sorrowful song—but in this dance or in this song there are fulfilled the most ancient rites of our conscience in the awareness of

being human and of believing in a common destiny.
—*Pablo Neruda,* poet and
Nobel Prize winner in Literature

✍

But I have discovered the secret that after climbing a great hill, one finds many more hills to climb. I have taken a moment here to rest, to steal a view of the glorious vista that surrounds me, to look back on the distance I have come. But I can rest only for a moment, for with my freedom comes responsibilities, and I dare not linger, for my long walk is not ended yet.
—*Nelson Mandela,* former president of South Africa and Nobel Peace Prize Laureate

SELECTED SOURCES

DEFINING SUCCESS

Pataki: Pataki, George. Commencement address, Colgate University, Hamilton, NY, May 17, 1998

Chopra: http://www.questforlife.com/success.html

Miller: http://quotes.prolix.nu/Struggle/Success/

Bronson: Bronson, Po. *What Should I Do With My Life?* New York: Random House, 2003.

Heaney: Heaney, Seamus. Commencement address, University of North Carolina, Chapel Hill, NC, May 12, 1996.

Hepburn: Hepburn, Katharine. *Me: Stories of My Life.* New York: Random House, Inc. 1991.

Emerson: Emerson, Ralph Waldo. *The Conduct of Life.* 1860.

Roosevelt: Roosevelt, Theodore. *An Autobiography.* Boston: Harvard University Press, 1913.

Allen: http://www.rkpuma.com/woody.htm

Mamet: Mamet, David. Commencement address, University of Vermont, Burlington, VT, May 28, 2004.

FINDING YOUR PASSION

Halberstam: Halberstam, David. Commencement address, Skidmore College, Saratoga, NY, May 22, 2004.

Torvalds: "An Interview with Linus Torvalds: Free, as in beer." By Joe Barr. *ITworld.com*, February 8, 2001.

Jobs: Steve Jobs, interview by Daniel Morrow, April 20, 1995, Computerworld Smithsonian Awards Program. http://americanhistory.si.edu/csr/comphist/sj1.html

Bon Jovi: Bon Jovi, Jon. Commencement address, Monmouth University, West Long Branch, NJ, May 16, 2001.

Fiorina: Fiorina, Carly. Commencement address, Massachusetts Institute of Technology, Cambridge, MA, June 2, 2000.

Woods: Tiger Woods, interview by Lorraine Hahn, *AsiaTalk*, CNN, March 17, 2003.

Page: "Google's Larry Page: Good Ideas Still Get Funded" *BusinessWeek Online* March 21, 2001. http://www. businessweek.com/bwdaily/ dnflash/mar2001/ nf20010313_831.htm

Damon: Matt Damon, interview by Ingrid Sischy, *Interview*, December 1997.

Bjork: Bjork, interview by Donna Karan, *Interview,* September 2001.

Szymborska: Szymborska, Wislawa, speech, "The Poet and the World" December 10, 1996

Brodsky: Brodsky, Joseph. Nobel Lecture in Literature, December 8, 1987.

Bradbury: Bradbury, Ray. Commencement address, California Institute of Technology, Pasadena, CA, May 20, 2000.

Dyson: "A conversation with Freeman Dyson." By Helen Joyce. *Plus* magazine, September 2003.

Mandela: Mandela, Nelson. *Long Walk to Freedom.* New York: Little, Brown Co., 1994.

Reeves: http://www. reeves-dogstar.com/ articles_realApril2001.html

Joel: Joel, Billy. Commencement address, Berklee College of Music, Boston, MA, May 1993.

Roddick: http://www. shareguide.com/Roddick.html

Alda: Alda, Alan. Commencement address, Connecticut College, New London, CT, May 1980.

Bogle: Bogle, John. Commencement address, Drexel University, Philadelphia, PA, June 14, 2003.

King: Luther King, Jr., Martin. *The Autobiography of Martin Luther King, Jr.* New York: Warner Books, 1998.

GETTING STARTED

Matthews: Matthews, Christopher. Commencement address, Hobart and William Smith Colleges, Geneva, NY, May 16, 2004.

Fellini: Frederico Fellini, interview by Toni Maraini, *Bright Lights Film Journal,* Issue 12, 1994.

Tesla: Nikola Tesla, *My Inventions,* edited by Ben Johnston. New York: Hart Brothers Pub, 1982.

Nassar: http://www.angelfire.com/film/russelcrowe/interview.htm

Rowling: J.K. Rowling, interview by Lindsey Fraser, *The Scotsman,* November 9, 2002.

Bhráonain: Eithne Ní Bhráonain, interview by *Inside Borders,* January 2001.

Auster: http://www.worldmind.com/Cannon/Culture/Interviews/auster.html

Tomlinson: Roy Tomlinson, interview by Sharon Gaudin, *Datamation,* July 16, 2002.

Newmark: Craig Newmark, interview by Nathan Kaiser, nPost.com, February 25, 2004.

Whitman: Meg Whitman, interview by Robert D. Hof, *BusinessWeek Online,* March 26, 2001.

Dangerfield: Dangerfield, Rodney. *It's Not Easy Bein' Me.* New York: HarperEntertainment, 2004.

Wozniak: Stephen Wozniak, interview by Jill Wolfson and John Leyba, *San Jose Mercury News,* February 1997.

Kroc: Kroc, Ray. *Grinding it Out: The Making of McDonald's.* New York: St. Martin's Press, 1990.

Kaplan: Kaplan, Stanley. *Test Pilot.* New York: Simon & Schuster, 2001.

Hasan: Sheeraz Hasan, interview by Hetal Adesara, Indiantelevision.com, September 30, 2003

James: P.D. James, interview by Jennifer Reese, *Salon.com,* February 26, 1998.

Sedaris: David Sedaris, interview by *The Onion A.V. Club,* August 29, 2001.

SETTING YOUR GOALS

Waitley: http://www.nonstopenglish.com/reading/quotations/k_Focus.asp

Jeter: Jeter, Derek. *The Life You Imagine.* New York: Crown Publishing, 2000.

Carpenter: "The Secrets of Their Success—and Yours," by Anna Muoio. *Fast Company* Magazine, June/July 1997.

Coffman: Coffman, Vance. Commencement address, Texas A&M University, College Station, TX, May 14, 2004.

Martin: http://www.chartattack.com/damn/2002/09/2001.cfm

Lucas: George Lucas, interview by the Academy of Achievement, June 19, 1999.

Schwarzenegger: Arnold Schwarzenegger, interview with Joel Holland http://www.streamingfuture.com/careers/transcripts/arnoldschwarzenegger.htm

Bloomberg: Bloomberg, Michael. *Bloomberg by Bloomberg*. New York: John Wiley & Sons, 1997.

Baxter: Stephen Baxter, interview by Tanya Brown, May 1999.

Shue: http://drdrew.com/DrewLive/article.asp?id=973

Bushnell: Candace Bushnell, interview by C.M. McDonald, June 2004.

Branson: http://www.woopidoo.com/business_quotes/authors/richard-branson-quotes.htm

Smith: http://www.femail.com.au/willsmith.htm

Viesters: Edward Viesters, interview by The Tech Museum of Innovation. October 26, 1998.

CULTIVATING CHARACTER

Orman: Orman, Suze. *The Courage to Be Rich*. New York: Riverhead, 1999.

Wall: Larry Wall, interview by Marjorie Richardson, *LinuxJournal.com*, May 1, 1999.

Winfrey: Winfrey, Oprah. Commencement address, Wellesley College, Wellesley, MA, May 30, 1997.

Jackson: Jackson, Samuel. Commencement address, Vassar College, Poughkeepsie, NY, May 23, 2004.

Hitchens: Hitchens, Christopher. *Letters to a Young Contrarian*. New York: Basic Books, 2001.

Reeve: Reeve, Christopher. Commencement address, Ohio State University, Columbus, OH, June 13, 2003.

Keitel: Harvey Keitel, interview by Oren Moverman, *Interview*, May 1999.

Glass: Ira Glass, interview by Zoë Francesca, *On The Page* magazine, Summer 2001.

Schultz: Schultz, Howard. *Pour Your Heart into It: How Starbucks Built a Company One Cup at a Time*. New York: Hyperion, 1999.

Lauder: Lauder, Leonard. Commencement address, Connecticut College, New London, CT, May 1989.

Bezos: Jeffrey Bezos, interview by the Academy of Achievement, San Antonio, TX, May 4, 2001.

Marsalis: Marsalis, Wynton. Commencement address, Connecticut College, New London, CT, May 2001.

Daft: http://www.iienetwork. org/?p=29253

Allison: Gabriel, Kalman. *Dear Kalman.* New York: HarperCollins, 1999.

Coppola: Sofia Coppola, interview by Chris Lee, *Blvd.,* April 2000.

Drucker: Peter Drucker, interview by *Information Outlook,* Vol. 6, No. 2, February 2002.

Mill: John Stuart Mill, *Autobiography,* ed. by John Robson New York: Penguin, 1990

Paglia: Camille Paglia, interview by Ingrid Sischy, *Interview,* July 1999.

Immelt: Immelt, Jeffrey. Commencement address, University of Miami, Miami, FL, May 9, 2003.

Hillary: Edmund Hillary, interview by *Scholastic.com,* November 1996.

Hurston: Hurston, Zora Neale. *Dust Tracks on a Road.* New York: Perennial, 1996.

Amis: http://www.altx.com/ int2/martin.amis.html

Hamilton: Scott Hamilton, interview by the Academy of Achievement, June 29, 1996.

Carrey: Dangerfield, Rodney. *It Ain't Easy Bein' Me.* New York: HarperEntertainment, 2004.

Forbes: Steve Forbes, interview by Joel Holland, *Streaming Futures,* New York, NY 2002.

Moore: Michael Moore, interview by Andrew Collins, *Guardian,* November 11, 2002.

BEING COMPETITIVE

Pinker: Brockman, John. Interview by John Brockman, *The Edge,* http://www.edge. org/3rd_culture/pinker/ pinker_p1.html

Couric: Katie Couric, interview by Larry King, *Larry King Weekend,* CNN, December 8, 2002.

Newman: Newman, Paul and A.E. Hotchner. *Shameless Exploitation in Pursuit of the Common Good.* New York: Nan A. Talese, 2003.

BEING DETERMINED

Tanaka: http://www.kyoto-np. co.jp/kp/english/special/ century/century05.html

Sevigny: Chloë Sevigny, interview by Ingrid Sischy, "She's Only Twenty-Five, But It's Already Hard To Imagine The Movies Without Her" *Interview,* September 2000.

Fry: Fry, Stephen. *Moab Is My Washpot: An Autobiography.* New York: Soho Press, 2000.

Smith: Smith, Frederick. "The Five Secrets of Entrepreneurial Success." Speech, Entrepreneurs Conference, Casa de Campo, Dominican Republic, February 2, 2001.

Dell: Dell, Michael and Catherine Fredman. *Direct From Dell: Strategies That Revolutionized an Industry.* New York: HarperBusiness, 2000.

Annan: Annan, Kofi. Commencement address, Massachusetts Institute of Technology, Cambridge, MA, June 6, 1997.

Streep: Streep, Meryl. Commencement address, University of New Hampshire, Durham, NH, May 24, 2003.

Foreman: Foreman, George. *George Foreman's Guide to Life.* New York: Simon & Schuster, 2002.

Murakami: Takashi Murakami, interview by Mako Wasaka, Brooklyn, N.Y., February 24, 2000.

Couric: Katie Couric, interview by Larry King, *Larry King Weekend,* CNN, December 8, 2002.

Mamet: http://www.rzuser. uni-heidelberg.de/~el6/ s_i_dream1.htm

Raskin: http://www.acm. org/ubiquity/interviews/ j_raskin_2.html

WORKING WITH OTHERS

McCain: McCain, John. Address, University of Southern California Ides of March Dinner, Los Angeles, CA, March 25, 2002.

Lawrence: Lawrence, Mary Wells. *A Big Life in Advertising.* New York: Knopf, 2002.

Heyward: Heyward, Andrew. Keynote address, Radio-Television News Directors Association and Foundation dinner, New York, NY, October 13, 2003.

Valenti: Jack Valenti, interview by Keith J. Winstein, *The Tech,* April 16, 2004.

Brown: Gurley Brown, Helen. *I'm Wild Again.* New York: Warner Books, 2001.

Vonnegut: Vonnegut, Kurt. Commencement address, Rice University, Houston, TX, May 9, 1998.

O'Reilly: O'Reilly, Bill. *The O'Reilly Factor.* New York: Broadway Books, 2002.

Letterman: David Letterman, interview by Ted Koppel, *Nightline UpClose*, ABC, July 9, 2002.

Rather: Rather, Dan. Lecture, Brown University, Providence, RI, April 16, 2001.

Feynman: Feynman, Richard. *The Pleasure of Finding Things Out.* New York: Perseus Publishing, 1999.

Matthews: Matthews, Christopher. Commencement address, Hobart and William Smith Colleges, Geneva, NY, May 16, 2004.

Crick: http://www.accessexcellence.org/AE/AEC/CC/crick.html

Dell: Michael Dell, interview with William J. Holstein, *Chief Executive*, 2003.

Franken: Franken, Al. Commencement address, Harvard University, Cambridge, MA, June 5, 2002.

Albright: Albright, Madeleine. *Madam Secretary.* New York: Miramax, 2003.

Dahl: Dahl, Roald. *Fantastic Mr. Fox.* New York: Random House, 1978, 1998.

LEADING OTHERS

Hillary: Edmund Hillary, interview by the Academy of Achievement, San Francisco, CA, November 16, 1991.

Immelt: Immelt, Jeffrey. Commencement address, University of Miami, Miami, FL, May 9, 2003.

Hoagland: http://www.laskerfoundation.org/awards/library/lumin_int_zp.html

Hefner: Trump, Donald. *The Way to the Top: The Best Business Advice I Ever Received.* New York: Crown Business, 2004.

Torvalds: "An Interview with Linus Torvalds: Free, as in beer." By Joe Barr. ITworld.com, February 8, 2001.

Biafra: Jello Biafra, interview by Jodi Vander Molen, *The Progressive*, February 2002.

WORKING HARD

Dick: http://www.philipkdickfans.com

Irving: Shindler, Dorman T. "John Irving Wrestles Fate," *Book Magazine*, July/August 2001.

Franken: "Franken's Beans," by Scott Vogel. *The Providence Phoenix*, June 20, 2003.

Dunlap: http://www.hedricksmith.com/site_bottomline/html/dunlap.html

TAKING RISKS

Shields: Shields, Mark. Commencement address, Hobart and William Smith Colleges, Geneva, NY, May 12, 2002.

Bushnell: http://www.thetech.org/revolutionaries/bushnell/i_a.html

Mamet: Mamet, David. Commencement address, University of Vermont, Burlington, VT, May 28, 2004.

Arnold: Arnold, Tom. *How I Lost 5 Pounds in 6 Years: An Autobiography*. New York: St. Martin's Press, 2002.

Lois: George Lois, interview by Les Simpson, *TimeOut New York*, issue 455, June 10, 2004.

Moore: Michael Moore, interview by Andrew Collins, *Guardian*, November 11, 2002.

Brooks: http://www.wga.org/craft/interviews/brooks.html

Kubrick: Kubrick, Stanley. Acceptance speech, Directors Guild of America Lifetime Achievement Award, 1997.

PROJECTING YOUR IMAGE

Lamb: Lamb, Brian. Commencement address, Saint Anselm College, Manchester, NH, May 22, 2004.

RoAne: RoAne, Susan. *How to Work a Room*. New York: HarperCollins, 2000.

Etcoff: Etcoff, Nancy. *Survival of the Prettiest: The Science of Beauty*. New York: Anchor Books/Doubleday, 2000.

Cole: Kenneth Cole, interviewed by Barbara Kruger, *Interview*, March 2004.

Gates: Bill Gates, interview by *Playboy*, July 1994.

Nicks: Stevie Nicks, interview by Sheryl Crow, *Interview*, May 2001.

Trump: Trump, Donald. *Trump: How to Get Rich*. New York: Random House, 2004.

Damon: Matt Damon, interview by Ingrid Sischy, *Interview*, December 1997.

Welch: Welch, Jack. *Jack: Straight From the Gut*. New York: Warner Business Books, 2001.

Madonna: http://www.nyrock.com/interviews/madonna_int.htm

Gray: Macy Gray, interview by Anita Sarko, *Interview*, November 2002.

Trump: Trump, Donald. *Trump: How to Get Rich.* New York: Random House, 2004.

Sheindlin: Sheindlin, Judy. *Beauty Fades, Dumb Is Forever: The Making of a Happy Woman.* New York: Cliff St. Books, 1999.

Paltrow: Gwyneth Paltrow, interview by Prairie Miller, *NYRock.com,* November 2001.

McNealy: Scott McNealy, interview by the *San Francisco Chronicle,* September 14, 2003.

Weill: http://www. chiefexecutive.net/weill.htm

Rosenberg: Rosenberg, William. *Time to Make the Donuts.* New York: Lebhar-Friedman, 2001.

Greenspan: Greespan, Alan. Commencement address, Harvard University, Cambridge, MA, June 10, 1999.

Owens: Queen Latifah, interview by *Jet,* September 18, 2000.

Grove: Andy Grove, interview by Walter Kiechel, *Harvard Management Update,* January 2003.

Raspberry: Raspberry, William. Commencement address, University of Delaware, Newark, DE, May 30, 1998.

Miller: Tanous, Peter. *Investment Gurus.* New York: Prentice Hall, 1997.

Clay: Andrew Dice Clay, interview by Jon Roig, *Arizona Daily Wildcat,* March 25, 1996.

DeLillo: Don, interview by Jörg Burger, *Die Zeit,* No. 42, October 8, 1998.

DiBaggio: Gabriel, Kalman. *Dear Kalman.* New York: HarperCollins, 1999.

Arnold: Arnold, Tom. *How I Lost 5 Pounds in 6 Years: An Autobiography.* New York: St. Martin's Press, 2002.

GETTING FEEDBACK

Clinton: Bill Clinton interview by Bill Paterniti, *Esquire,* December 2000.

Torvalds: "An Interview with Linus Torvalds: Free, as in beer." By Joe Barr. ITworld. com, February 8, 2001.

O'Brien: O'Brien, Conan. Commencement address, Harvard University, Cambridge, MA, June 7, 2000.

Newmark: Craig Newmark, interview by Nathan Kaiser, nPost.com, February 25, 2004.

Darwin: Charles Darwin, *The Life and Letters of Charles Darwin,* edited by Francis Darwin; New York: Prometheus Books, 2000.

Brin: "A Long Lonely Road: Some Informal Advice to New Authors," by David Brin, http://www.davidbrin.com.

Bellow: Bellow, Saul. Nobel Banquet Speech, Stockholm, Sweden, December 10, 1976.

BEING FEARLESS

Ignatieff: Ignatieff, Michael. Commencement address, Whitman College, Walla Walla, WA, May 23, 2004.

Rubin: Rubin, Robert. Commencement address, Harvard University, Cambridge, MA, June 7, 2001.

Armstrong: "Back in the Saddle," by Lance Armstrong. *Forbes,* December 3, 2001.

Poitier: Poitier, Sidney. *The Measure of a Man: A Memoir.* New York: Simon & Schuster, 2000.

Lederberg: Joshua Lederberg, interview by Lev Pevzner, *www.almaz.com,* March 20, 1996.

Hepburn: Hepburn, Katharine. *Me: Stories of My Life.* Haynes Publications, 1993.

Steinem: Steinem, Gloria. Commencement address, Tufts University, Medford, MA, May 17, 1987.

Nader: Nader, Ralph. Commencement address, Bucknell University, Lewisburg, PA, May 23, 2004.

Branson: Branson, Richard. *Losing My Virginity: The Autobiography.* Crown: New York, 1998.

Clinton: Clinton, Hillary Rodham. *Living History.* New York: Simon & Schuster, 2003.

Rushdie: Rushdie, Salman. Commencement address, Bard College, Annandale-on-Hudson, NY, May 25, 1996.

SURVIVING SETBACKS

Fuller: http://www.futurehi.net/docs/Bucky_Interview01.html

Keillor: Keillor, Garrison. Commencement address, Princeton University, Princeton, NJ, June 5, 2001.

Malkovich: "Independent on Sunday" London, April 5, 1992.

Clinton: Bill Clinton, interview by Bill Paterniti, *Esquire,* December 2000.

Lennon: Sheff, David. *All We Are Saying: The Last Major Interview with John Lennon and Yoko Ono.* New York: St. Martin, 2000.

Graham: Graham, Katharine. *Personal History.* New York: Alfred A. Knopf, 1997.

Travolta: John Travolta, interview by Erika Hernandez, www.aboutfilm.com, 2004.

Anderson: Pamela Anderson, interview by Hal Rubenstein, *Interview,* November 1998.

Mehta: Deepa Mehta, interview by Wyndham Wise, *Take One,* September-November 2002.

Salk: Jonas Salk, interview by the Academy of Achievement, San Diego, CA, May 16, 1991.

Hellmuth: Phil Hellmuth, interview by Saira Stewart, *ABCNews.com,* February 25, 2002.

DeGeneres: Ellen DeGeneres, interview by Alanis Morissette, *Interview,* July 2003.

Greene: http://www.pbs.org/wgbh/nova/elegant/greene.html

Kubrick: Stanley Kubrick, interview by Tim Cahill, *Rolling Stone,* August 27, 1987.

Lahiri: http://www.pifmagazine.com/SID/598/

MANAGING STRESS

Stewart: Stewart, Jon. Commencement address, The College of William and Mary, Williamsburg, VA, May 16, 2004.

Gosling: James Gosling, interview by Bill Venners, *JavaWorld,* June 2001.

Bezos: Jeffrey Bezos, interview by the Academy of Achievement, San Antonio, TX, May 4, 2001.

Pulsifer: http://www.stresslesscountry.com/onequestion/

Kazin: Alfred Kazin, interview by Roger Bishop, www.bookpage.com, 1996.

Giuliani: Rudolph Giuliani, interview by the Academy of Achievement, San Anton, TX, May 3, 2003.

Maharaj: Swami Veda Bharati Maharaj, interview by Lorraine Hahn, *TalkAsia,* CNN, May 15, 2002.

STAYING SUCCESSFUL

Gerhart: http://www.worldofquotes.com

Mayer: "In It for the Long Haul," by Rex Rutkoski, *The Inside Connection,* www.insidecx.com.

Orcharton: http://www. sie.ed.ac.uk/resources/ Marilyn%20Orcharton.htm

Lear: Lear, Norman. Commencement address, USC Annenberg School for Communication, Los Angeles, CA, May 16, 2003.

Stevenson: "Four Keys of Enduring Success: How High Achievers Win," by Martha Lagace. *HBS Working Knowledge*, June 24, 2002.

Siebert: Siebert, Muriel. Commencement address, Case Western Reserve University, Cleveland, OH, May 17, 1998.

Williams: Jody Williams, interview by Rachel Stohl, *ADM Online*, February 4, 1999.

Mandela: Mandela, Nelson. *Long Walk to Freedom*. New York: Little, Brown Co., 1994.

PERMISSIONS

Special thanks to the following for their permission to republish quotes in this book:

Jobs (p. 19): interview by Dan Morrow for the Computerworld Honors Foundation

Schwarzenegger (p. 58): interview by Joel Holland for the career exploration show, Streaming Futures, which is part of Nortel Kidz Online

Bloomberg (pp. 60–61): *Bloomberg on Bloomberg* by Michael Bloomberg. Copyright © 1997 Michael R. Bloomberg. Reprinted with permission of John Wiley & Sons, Inc.

Forbes (p. 93): interview by Joel Holland for the career exploration show, Streaming Futures, which is part of Nortel Kidz Online

Dell (p. 105): Edited excerpt from pages 4–5, as submitted, from *Direct from Dell: Strategies that Revolutionized an Industry* by Michael Dell with Catherine Friedman. Copyright © 1999 by Michael Dell. Reprinted with permission of HarperCollins, Inc.

Branson (p. 198–99): From *Losing My Virginity* by Richard Branson, copyright © 1998 by Richard Branson. Used by permission of Times Business, a division of Random House, Inc., and by permission of Virgin Books Ltd.